Endorsements

"Danny Bader's story is wonderfully told with rich characters, honest self-reflection, and valuable insight."

David Allen,
Bestselling author of *Getting Things Done,*
The Art of Stress-Free Productivity

"If there is one self-improvement motivational book you read this year this is the one! Danny Bader has written a page turner of a book that is powerful, heartfelt and could just change how you think about life. Look over your shoulder Robin Sharma and Deepak Chopra you now have Danny Bader galloping up behind you!"

Shawn Doyle, CSP, Speaker and trainer
Author of *Jumpstart Your Motivation* and *MO!*

"A book of wisdom, tenderly written, filled with characters you will care for and dialogue that captures our humanity. Jackrabbit will never mean the same thing for you."

John P. Schuster
Author of *The Power of You Past*

D1490523

"Back To Life is a compelling story, based on a real-life event, sprinkled liberally with insightful lessons for every reader. It is impossible to read this book and not reflect on your own life, values, and guiding principles. In a time when people are often distracted by the 'busy-ness' of life, this book offers pearls of wisdom to remember what is most important on the journey."

Kathleen Stinnett, Founder of FutureLaunch
Author of *The Extraordinary Coach:*
How the Best Leaders Help Others Grow

Back to Life

The Path of Resilience

Based on a true story

DANNY BADER

Dedication

To Lisa, Luke, Joey and Lizzy...my life is enriched with you in it.

To all of my family and friends that have loved and encouraged me and continue to do so...this story is for you.

Be well.

Danny

Contents

Foreword

Danny Bader invites readers of *Back To Life: The Path of Resilience* to come face to face with the wonders of their developing personalities—and then to offer an "Amen!" So many beautiful life lessons emerge from his book and help readers develop their own vision for a meaningful life. One striking insight shared by Bader is to learn the difference between living and being alive.

Underscoring the power of one's own story and the courage of sharing it with others, Bader employs humor, inspiration, and hope to invite readers to go deeper in finding the answer to the great question: "What should I do with my life?" The principles of life-long learning that Bader calls Jackrabbit are provocative yet not overwhelming, simple yet not simplistic, and spiritual yet not preachy. Coming to terms with a life-altering event, Bader helps us discover the wisdom that reverses the dictum of "Don't just sit there, do something" to "Don't just do something, sit there." The dynamic change Bader undergoes, similar to the "fictional" character in the book, is one that will inspire readers to live life more artfully, generously, and passionately.

Back To Life: The Path of Resilience is an engaging read, and will leave you a different person, having spent time with a wonderful story about the journey all of us are on. Bader creatively invites us to intersect our stories with his—and the results may be as rich, happy, and fulfilling as his.

James J. Greenfield, OSFS
Provincial, Oblates of St. Francis de Sales Wilmington, DE

Acknowledgements

I'd like to thank and acknowledge all of my family and friends for their love and support throughout my life...I love you.

To the many colleagues I've met over the years—thanks for your friendship, encouragement and contribution to my growth.

To all those who've attended my workshops & keynotes, read my books, and listened to my Back To Life podcast. I'm thankful to support you on your journey of life, and humbled by the feedback you provide. Press on...run the race...fight the good fight.

A special thanks to my editor, Sue, for her humor, coaching, vision and discipline; and to Harry for helping me with this story at the beginning.

Thanks to Christy and Martha for their insight on cover design and book launch, and to my longtime friend, Fran, for her wonderful discussion questions at the end of the book. Thanks to Brittany for making all this "work."

To Elyse, AJ, Rory and the Brand Builders Group team— thanks for your "push" with my brand.

And to a few of my friends who have passed on:

To Bruce and Stew, who were—and are—with me on this journey, thanks for staying close in Spirit.

To "Angel," keep an eye on us all. Miss you, buddy.

Preface

Each of us has a story—an interpretation of the events that have occurred for us up to this point. Some tell their story. Some write their story. Some suppress their story. This story, originally published with the title *Back from Heaven's Front Porch*, is a vital piece of my story. It was published in 2012, some 20 years after the accident that serves as the story's foundation.

As I've grown in my work, I've worked to gain clarity on my brand, and what I'm passionate about. It's simple, I literally came *back to life*, and identified powerful principles to apply to create joy in this life, and to build resilience through the difficult times.

While you have likely not experienced dying then coming back…I'd encourage you to see it differently. Each day you do come back to life and two vital questions to ask and answer (the power is in the answering) are:

#1   What am I up to creating in my life?

#2   How am I going about doing this? And where must I grow stronger?

This second edition, titled *Back To Life*, was published to strengthen the book title and cover to better reflect the story of Jake—one of resilience—as well as to add a final chapter as Jake's life has unfolded since the accident many years ago. Many of you have asked, "What happened after Jake got home?" I've added a new final chapter to address this question, as well as potential book club discussion questions to accommodate the many requests I've received over the years.

The story is a work of fiction based on real events, and is told through the perspective of a young man named Jake (a character whose struggle is modeled after mine). *Back To Life* welcomes us into Jake's world at a very pivotal point in his young life; a life that was void of any real challenges…that is, until July 28, 1992, and the months following. When asked to explain the principles by which they live, many people cannot answer quickly, or easily. They usually say they've never really thought about them. Jake no longer has this option. In his desperate quest to survive, he is forced to seek and understand—and choose to implement—the principles by which he will go from just living to being ALIVE. Jake needs a huge dose of resilience as he seeks to survive, and grow through this tragedy. He gets this chance when he meets a friendly stranger while body surfing the waves of the Outer Banks in North Carolina.

Over the years since the initial release of this story I have led many workshops and delivered many talks on the principles within this story known as jackrabbit…or *jckrbbt* for short. Jckrbbt is a lifestyle; a set of principles that guide how one lives. I've been thankful for the tremendous amount of feedback you've given me about the value you've gained in life by adopting some, or all of the *jckrbbt* principles.

As you read Jake's story, you will likely make some connections with Jake, Paul, Brendan, and the other characters he meets that offer him *jckrbbt*—the simple set of principles that can liberate him from the dark spiral his life is taking onto the path of resilience. Over the years I have enjoyed hearing from readers about the characters they love, and about which principle of jckrbbt is meaningful to them at this point in their life. The intention I hold for you is that you'll experience the same, and this will support you, and you'll begin experimenting with the *jckrbbt* approach to assist you in growing from just living to being ALIVE to greater levels of happiness and fulfillment. This is my vision for you. Enjoy!

1

Why Did I Have to Come Back?

"We are not certain, we are never certain."
–Albert Camus

Why is there no blood?

That was my only thought as I stared at the two black holes in my boots. An ambulance had screeched to the curb a few minutes ago, and a heavy man in a blue uniform had run across the burnt grass. He'd shoved me out of the way as he bent to work on my friend Brian. The EMT had pulled medical gear from a red case. His partner had glanced up at the flashing lights of the police car, speaking into her hand-held radio.

Steve, the third member of our work crew and Brian's brother, stood over the EMT, watching closely. I'd crawled away and propped myself against a scratchy brown picket fence. That's when I'd noticed the two black holes in my work boots. *Why is there no blood?*

I'd never considered what it would feel like to have 10,000 volts of electricity shoot through my body. At least that's what most of the people—lawyers and electric company folks—told me afterwards. Between 10,000 and 13,000 volts, they said, ripped down the ladder when it hit the wire. I know I wasn't thinking about the numbers as the hot July wind blew across the dry grass that day sixteen years ago.

The EMTs were still working on Brian as I pulled off my boots, then my socks, and saw that the black holes went right through my skin. *Why is there no blood?* Later, the first doctor, at the first hospital, explained that the electricity burned the ends of the blood vessels—"cauterized them" is what he said. The holes I was peering into were the result of the electricity bursting through my skin in its natural need to escape my body.

The first ambulance rushed off, sirens screeching. Some kids rode up on their bikes. "Mister, what's wrong with your feet?" I didn't have an answer. Two new EMTs came up to me and it wasn't long before I was on my way to the hospital, too. That's when I met that first doctor.

I don't remember his name, only that he was young, and he was wrong. Right about my feet, but very wrong about what happened to me that day. He arrogantly stated that I'd had a loss of consciousness for a period of minutes; LOC is how it was written in the medical report.

I knew better. I hadn't lost consciousness at all. My 28-year-old body may have stopped working, but not my mind, not my soul. I swear that at first I was screaming at Steve to go to Brian, though later on Steve told me I didn't make a sound.

"You weren't breathing and you didn't have a heartbeat," he told me afterwards. "Your eyes were rolled back into your head. Your lips and mouth were covered in foam."

Steve had tried CPR on me but it didn't work; he said my chest just rose and fell as he blew his breath into my mouth. He couldn't find a pulse, couldn't get a response. So he went to work on Brian. He'd given me up for dead.

Me? I know nothing about this. You see I was no longer there.

I'd gone away. To where, you're wondering. Well, to this day I'm not sure, but I do know it was to a place where I was enveloped and surrounded...in something, some encompassing blackness. Although these words don't really capture it. I don't know how to describe it in our language. Perhaps saying I was embraced in love and peace? But it wasn't a love and peace like we're used to. No, it was a love and peace that I don't believe exist here on earth. Close... maybe. I'll tell you more about this later.

Then at a critical moment, I'd come back. I don't know how to explain it any other way. I *wasn't* there and then I *was*. My muscles weren't working too well, but I'd managed to crawl over to Steve, who was doing CPR on Brian. Steve kept doing the chest compressions. I'd puff into Brian's mouth every few seconds. His breath smelled like the tuna fish sandwich I'd brought for him that day. You have to start eating healthier, man, I'd said. Only I guess it didn't make much difference.

Then the first EMTs had arrived. The kids on the bikes came and went. I was taken to the hospital, too. Steve came into my room eventually and all he could say was, "We killed Brian, Jake. We killed him."

I think about that day often. Why'd I come back? Why did I have to come back? Why didn't I stay where I was, in that peaceful place? Or go even farther away?

I was sure, you see, that God got it wrong. That it was me who was supposed to die that day. And it wasn't "we" who killed Brian. It was just me.

2

Rock Bottom Is a Hell of a Place

"The present will not long endure."
—Pindar

I had been lying in the first hospital for a couple of hours when my mom showed up. She leaned in and stroked my hair. "Why did you kiss me last night?" she asked.

The kiss had been a surprise for both of us. We'd been having a fight for the past two weeks, and had barely spoken. She had gotten on my back about not being able to commit to my on-again, off-again girlfriend, Lauren, whom I'd been dating for six years. I was 28, living at home, not using my college degree. I owed my uncle ten grand for a loan I'd used to start up a business that was now failing. To make spending money, I'd been working as a bartender and even offered to help my buddy Steve with his roofing business a few days a week.

But last night, for some reason, I'd kissed my mom goodnight. I don't know why. At the hospital, she wondered out loud if I'd had some insight that I might not be around to kiss her goodnight for much longer. I didn't have an answer to that, just like I didn't have answers to a lot of questions.

After several hours in the first hospital I was flown by helicopter to a trauma center better equipped to treat my injuries. The next week was spent in that hospital with tubes sticking out of most of my body, secured with medical tape. Machines and monitors standing around my bed became my constant companions—hissing, sucking and dinging noises filling the room.

People streamed in and out of my room—cardiologists for my heart, plastic surgeons for my feet, and psychiatrists, family, friends and priests for my head. Meaning well, they delivered typical post-tragedy thoughts: "So terrible, you're lucky to be here." "Boy, did you dodge a bullet." "I guess God has a plan for you." "I'm here if you need me." "Anything you need, just call."

My feet hurt badly after they cut out all the dead tissue. Debridement is what they called it. Dr. Murray even took a sliver of skin from my left hip and wrapped it around my left big toe. When I lay in bed my skin hurt so much that the weight of the sheet was enough to get me buzzing the nurse for another Percocet. Lauren thought I was being grumpy.

One day when I was alone in the room, I felt a presence. I thought it was more likely Brian come back to visit me than God. The windows were closed and there wasn't any air conditioning on, but one of the Mylar balloons was moving back and forth in response to my thoughts. I told my family and friends about it afterwards, and they said the medications made me hallucinate. I was sure Brian had been there. But whether he came to comfort or condemn me, I wasn't sure at the time.

I left the hospital for good at the end of that week about ten pounds lighter. I was scared.

I spent the next two months at my mom and dad's house, where I'd been living as a way to save money. At first, I welcomed the near-constant attention. I found it very easy to not have to make any decisions. Well, I did have to decide whether to get out of bed in the mornings, and the answer wasn't always yes. The nightmares were so bad that I barely slept, and I used that as an excuse to avoid company. All I had to say was "I don't feel so good, Mom," and she'd turn away everyone, including my brothers and sisters, and even intercept calls from my best friend Joe and my former-or-maybe current girlfriend, Lauren. I just couldn't stand the pity in their eyes every time they looked at me, and the way they very carefully avoided talking about anything real when I was around. I much preferred to be alone.

Mom and Dad gave me some space, but it wasn't long before their parenting instincts took over, and the gentle prods of "You should really get out of the house," and "When do you think you'll be ready to go back to work?" and "Joe called again. Don't you think it's time you talked to him?" gradually became more insistent. So I agreed to get out of the house more. And I did. I visited Brian's grave once with my Mom. Then I dropped her off at home and drove straight to the closest bar and stayed until it closed. I switched bars every night so no one would know for sure where I was. But eventually one of my brothers would find me and try to get me to return home. It became an unwelcomed ritual. That's when I started driving to the bars two towns over.

I kept replaying the accident in my mind, and the sense of inadequacy that had been brewing inside me for years got even worse. Everything that hadn't been working in my life before the accident was a hundred times worse. I was a failure at everything I'd tried. I was just a few years shy of my thirtieth birthday and still didn't have a real job. Despite thinking that, maybe I loved Lauren, something kept me from taking the steps towards a deeper, stronger relationship.

In short, though the physical pain gradually eased, I felt worse and worse every day.

Back when I was six, I remember sitting on the curb of my church in Towson, Maryland, telling anyone who passed that I was going to be a priest. During college I found myself attracted to the psychology and philosophy classes—always wanting to know how and why we functioned the way we did. Now, I stopped going to church. Vodka—not God—had become my sole refuge. I tried going to a psychiatrist, several, in fact, in succession. The third one looked a lot like Steven Spielberg. But after I left every session, I'd stop by a bar on my way back to my car so I could "adjust" before going home.

One night at a bar, I even tried some "diet pills" a friend gave me, which I guess were probably speed or something. I got so stoned that one of my brothers freaked out when he finally tracked me down, and he came down on me hard for playing around with that stuff.

"You're becoming a real screw up, Jake. You know that?" he said. "You have so much going for you and you're messing it all up."

3

Run

"Adversity is the first path to truth."

–Lord Byron

I could see that I was hurting my family by not healing as fast as they wanted me to. *They just don't understand what I'm going through, I thought.* And there was no use trying to explain everything. My brother was right, I was screwing up.

And that's how, one fine morning about two months after leaving the hospital, I came to think of one thing I *could* do right: I could go away so I wouldn't drag anyone else down with me. I decided to run.

-9-

But where? I chose my destination: the Outer Banks of North Carolina, a beautiful slice of nature positioned amidst the shifting tides of the Atlantic and right smack in the middle of one of Mother Nature's favorite paths of fury.

The conversation with my Mom went like this.

"I'm just going to go down there for a few days, Mom. I need to get away for a bit."

"Okay Jake, I understand. But why not just go to Avalon, you love it there and it's much closer. Why drive eight or ten hours all the way to North Carolina where you're away from us and don't know a soul?"

"That's the whole point, Mom. I'm surrounded by people who know me and know what happened. I need a break."

"A break? Jake, it seems to me, and the others, that you're not letting any of us in. You spend so much time alone, and turn down many of our invitations to talk or just do something like dinner or shopping or watching a Phillies game. I guess I'm alright with you needing to go, but it really doesn't seem like I have a choice. But promise me you'll be careful."

I forced a smile and made the promise. Before I left, I called all my siblings to tell them I was leaving, and made sure to throw in a quick "love ya" at the end of each conversation. I did the same with Mom and Dad. I wanted to make sure that they would remember what might be our last words. *If only they knew what I was really thinking.*

On the way south the next day, I decided to connect with a piece of my past, stopping to see my old friend Marty — "Father" to most who knew him. I'd met Marty in 1981 when I was a freshman and he was a teacher at a small Catholic college near Allentown, Pennsylvania. Back then, I was still wondering whether to fulfill my childhood dream of becoming a priest.

Now, I had a vague thought that maybe talking to Marty would help me sort things out.

Over our dinner of chicken parmesan and red wine we spoke about my accident.

"It just doesn't make sense to me that God would let something like this happen," I said.

"Let?"

I shrugged, pouring myself some more wine. "He screwed this one up, Marty. Big time. Brian had three kids, the youngest only a few months old. I just have a sometime girlfriend."

Marty nodded.

"And my mom wonders why I don't feel like going to church." I sipped my wine. "This sucks."

"This does suck."

I coughed, choking on my fettuccine.

"It's good to be mad at God, and He's good with it," Marty said.

"Really?"

"Sure. You see Jake, when you're mad at someone—like the way you're pissed at God—at least there's still a relationship, it's just in a negative state."

"Negative." I rolled my eyes. "I guess that's one way to put it."

"You and I both know you need to keep your relationship with Him. You're mad at Him for the same reason many folks are. They want God to control everything from up there in his big chair, waving his wand and pulling the strings. But that's not the way it works. You go ahead and be mad at Him, but just be open to where that may lead you."

I pondered those words that night. "Open to where it may lead you." Right now, it was leading me towards the Outer

Banks of North Carolina, a journey I didn't really expect to return from.

The next morning as my pickup truck pulled out of Marty's drive, I glanced at the large figure dressed in black in my rearview mirror. And just as with all the goodbyes I'd said yesterday, I wondered if I'd see him again.

4

Date with a Garden Hose

"Nothing is worth more than this day."
–Johann von Goethe

On the third morning in North Carolina, I woke, for the countless time, from dreams of soundless screams, smells of burning flesh, and cries of anguish. A now-familiar figure, the coroner, had been there too. I made myself a cup of coffee then sat on the wooden roof deck of my one-story beachfront motel, studying the ocean, feet propped on the railing. I had an odd, but clear sensation about what I had to do. I'd discovered nothing. The ocean's roar didn't hold the secret to life. God wasn't speaking to me through waves and sand. Brian was still dead. I was alive. Booze wasn't much of a refuge any more.

I arose then followed the sandy path beside the road to a brightly painted building I'd scoped out the previous day. The sun bouncing off the yellow exterior of the only local grocery/hardware store blinded me. I pulled open the peeling, white wooden door and was greeted with the scent of sun block. Walking past the rows of t-shirts, hats, and shell necklaces I found what I was looking for, garden hoses.

I sized them up, thinking about how much smaller the diameter was than that of the car's exhaust pipe. *Maybe duct tape would keep it in place.* I didn't want to have to bother with anything more elaborate. *I wondered if the rubber material would melt too quickly?* There were some that had reinforced heavy plastic collars at the ends, and maybe that would do the trick. I didn't need a fifty foot hose, the shortest, at fifteen feet, would do the trick. I then had the choice of green or black. Whatever I'd anticipated in my life, it wasn't having to decide the color of a garden hose, that I wasn't going to use in any garden.

I reached for a green one—then yanked my hand back. A woman strolled by the end of the aisle holding a rake and nodded politely at me. I let out a sigh, grabbed the hose, found the duct tape in a different part of the store, and headed to the front of the store. At the counter I picked up a bottle of sun block, and then placed it back on the rack—not going to be needing that any more.

Back at the motel I chugged a beer, then jumped into my truck, throwing the hose into the bed. I drove through the beach entrance past the dunes, pulled back the 4-wheel drive lever, and drove along the water's edge about a half-mile to the north. I found a deserted spot and made a hard right turn, shut off the engine, and stared at the ocean. And I wept. I wept loud and long.

I guess it was hours later when I drove back to the motel. I showered, pulled on jeans and a black long sleeve t-shirt, and left my room.

In search of false courage, I headed to the bar a few blocks away. Only three days and the bartenders already knew my name… and I knew theirs… The bar was about half full and the guy from last night was playing his guitar—same cowboy hat and boots. I slid onto a stool.

The bartender approached, "What do you need, Jake?"

"Just a Miller Lite, please, Bob."

The cowboy guitarist was actually pretty good, his voice taking the tone of the different artists whose songs he played. The crowd grew over time.

I started talking to a young guy. When the singer finished, the kid stood and said, "Wanna smoke some weed? I got some pretty good stuff."

"Yeah, sure." Something inside me didn't want to go, but I followed him anyway. We went into the parking lot. The rest of the night rolled past with music, a little dancing, and more beers.

Later, much later, I stumbled back across the gravel parking lot toward the motel. Nothing—not the booze, not the weed, not the singer, not the crowd—had been able to wipe the vision of the garden hose completely from my mind.

As I turned the corner of the building, I noticed a phone booth sitting under a street lamp. The phone booth was definitely not there when I arrived. Fresh, bright red paint confirmed this. There were no scratches, no names or numbers of star-crossed lovers etched in the middle of a heart. It was new. I thought through my beer, pot, and tequila-clouded mind. This is *very* weird. Cities are tearing down phone booths, not putting them up.

As if I was being drawn by someone, or something, I entered the booth and removed the receiver, placing the cool black phone to my ear. I dialed a number I knew by heart, my fingers moving unconsciously across the numbers, and waited.

"Hello."

I paused, my hand suddenly sweaty.

"Hello?" the voice repeated.

"Hi, Mom, it's me."

"Hello, Jake. I'm just so happy you called. When are you coming home? Everyone else was over for dinner tonight and we already miss you. We can't wait to see you again."

Tears rolled down my cheeks as I tried forcing the words past my tightening throat. "I'll be home in a few days," I said. I wasn't sure whether I was lying or not.

What we spoke of over the next few minutes, I'm not sure. The only things I remember are my mom's happy tone and saying goodbye before placing the phone back in its cradle.

Slowly I shuffled in the direction of my room, wiping my face with my sleeve. *So happy you called, Mom had said. We miss you. Can't wait to see you again.* Was it true? I'd been convinced before I left that everyone in my life would be much better off without me in theirs. She'd probably heard in my voice that I'd been drinking. But she hadn't scolded, hadn't told me I was messing up yet again. Just so *happy... see you again.*

After a few steps I stopped, as if a large hand had me in its grasp. Turning back to the phone booth, its shiny metal and clear glass glistening under the lone streetlight, I felt a slight smile crease my face. I passed my truck with the hose still lying in the back and put the key in the motel door. I slid off my shoes, laid down on the bed, and to my surprise fell asleep almost instantly.

5

Open to Where It May Lead

"The way to see by Faith is to shut the eye of Reason."
–Benjamin Franklin

When I woke the next morning, my fog had slightly lifted. I splashed water on my face, threw an old grey t-shirt on with my swim trunks, and headed for the beach. Passing through the motel breezeway, my leather flip-flops smacking against the pavement, I glanced down and imagined that even the scars on my feet looked a little tanner, blending more with my natural skin color.

The sunlight bounced off the ocean and, except for two seagulls to my right searching for their breakfast, I was alone.

Perfect, I thought, just me. I shed my shirt and flipped off my sandals, then walked to where the soft white sand turned gray and smooth. The water was cool but not cold. God, it feels great today. Breathing in deeply, I smelled the distinct aroma of the ocean and its inhabitants. Miniature rainbows appeared as the spray blew back toward the ocean when waves began to break.

Grinning, I looked up at an approaching wave and gasped, jumping back. A bald head emerged from the foaming white water, followed by a wrinkled face and glistening grey-haired chest.

"Whew, what a ride." The man wiped his eyes and struggled to get his footing. "Nothing like a little early-morning dip to get the heart pumpin' and the soul stirred."

We stared, I at him and he at me. Where'd he come from? There were no other clothes on the beach. Exactly how long had he been riding that wave?

"So what do you think? You wanna ride some of these babies?" He turned, pointing at three head-high walls of water approaching. "Or," he grinned, "are you just out here to pee?" He turned toward the approaching waves and dove under, and then, popping up, began a smooth, freestyle stroke.

Looking around for a moment, and letting out a laugh, I dove under in the direction of this mysterious old body-surfer.

We floated next to one another.

"My name's Jake." I got to my feet, the water receding to my chest, and extended my hand.

"Hi, Jake, nice to meet you. I'm Paul. Hey, here comes a good one."

I pushed off the sandy bottom and made two strokes as the wave began to lift my body and welcome me into its momentum. My arms dropped to my side as I began to slide down the face of the wave heading to my right. The wave released me as

I pulled up my shorts and stood in the knee deep ocean quite a distance from where I'd just taken off.

Paul slid by me. "Whoa!" His head shimmered and his blue swim trunks were barely visible under the wave.

"So Jake—you did say your name's Jake, right?" A wave slapped his chest.

"Yeah."

"So, what is it that brings a young man like you down here to this bit of paradise?"

"I'm not really sure—" I gazed along the foamy waves lapping the shoreline "—now."

Paul stared straight into my eyes. "What do you mean *now*."

"Well. I came down here to do something." I glanced from Paul to the open water.

Paul said nothing, creating a silence that made my stomach tighten.

"But now I'm not sure I want to do it. It may not be the answer I'm looking for. I'm kind of mixed up."

"What is it you want to do?" Paul waited.

"Not sure."

"Then what do you want your future to look like?" He glanced from me to the water as we slowly made our way out to catch another wave.

"Not sure of that either."

"Then that's probably what you'll wind up with."

"What's that?"

"Not sure." Paul smiled, cupping some water in his hands and splashing his face. "I've seen far too many people not sure what they want from life—or where they're headed. And you know what they end up with?"

I shrugged, shaking my head.

"They get to a place in life—a meaningless job or relationship, retirement, the loss of a loved one, or perhaps a seemingly significant birthday, usually around forty or fifty—and they ask themselves, 'How did I end up here?' The answer comes slowly, a whisper, often accompanied by some twinge in the belly. It comes from deep inside and it says, 'Not sure.'"

"Life's really just a cycle of transitions, Jake. People who know this and put some effort into these transitions, those that actually create the other side of the transition, are the ones who, in my humble opinion, seem fulfilled. The others...," he chuckled "well, they just bitch too much!"

I wasn't sure how to reply. I'd just met this guy five minutes ago and already he was giving me life advice. Luckily, a big wave saved me from having to respond. Our next ride ended with us standing again in knee-deep water. Paul wiggled his pinky into his ear, shook his head, then said he'd had enough and walked down the beach.

"Yeah, whatever." I replied coldly.

It was an odd conversation. I rode a few more waves, but bodysurfing wasn't much fun alone. I scanned the beach for a glimpse of Paul but he was gone. Fifteen minutes later I was back in my room drinking a beer. After two more I lay back down and fell asleep.

Late in the afternoon, after a fitful nap and way too many nasty dreams, I became pissed off at my inertia. I thought again about the hose and duct tape waiting for me in the truck, but I couldn't face them just yet. So I grabbed a beer and headed back to the beach.

The sun hung behind me as I strolled toward an ocean whose waves had now flattened out. The beach had always been one of my favorite places, a peaceful place where the feeling of the sand, either hot or cool, on my bare feet allowed me to relax.

I caught sight of somebody sitting on the shore, his outstretched legs crossed at the ankles, staring at the ocean as though studying something very interesting. It was Paul.

I wasn't sure I wanted to talk to him again, but I didn't want to be alone just then, either. So I walked down to join him.

"Hey, Paul."

He looked up, rising to his feet brushing the sand from his tan shorts.

"Hi, Jake."

"I'm, uh, I'm sorry if I seemed a little pissed this morning, but I've got some baggage I'm trying to deal with." I looked down into the mouth of my beer. "I guess you were just trying to help, but so have a lot of people and I guess I just get a bit edgy sometimes."

Paul shifted his gaze from the vastness of the ocean.

"Forget about it, Jake. People always tell me I move too fast and say whatever's on my mind without thinking first. Not such a good practice in some instances, especially when you first meet someone. Could we start over?"

I began to relax. "Sure, Paul. It's alright. So, where you from? Why are you down here?"

"Let's sit for a moment." Paul sat back down, stretching his legs out and leaning back. "Let's see, where do I start?"

"How about at the beginning." I wiggled the beer bottle into the sand and sat down next to him.

"You already know that I can go off on tangents, so I'll make this very short. I'm a small town boy, from rural Ohio. Lived there my whole life except for the years I was in Korea." He glanced at me. "During the war, you know? I fell in love with and married the girl next door. Her name was Virginia, but we all called her Ginny. We had two beautiful daughters and were very happy until two years ago when Ginny died. The two of us used to come down here every October. And now I still come so I can spend more time with Ginny.

"Sorry for your loss, Paul."

"Yeah, thanks. It's a loss alright. Ginny was my best friend. God bless her, though, she was always positive and giving, even toward the end. She used to joke with our grandchildren and color pictures with them."

"She sounds wonderful."

"Wonderful isn't the half of it. Losing her was, and still is, the toughest thing I've ever done." Paul stretched and then crossed his legs. "So, what about you? Wanna tell me anymore about who Jake is, and why you're here?" He smiled. "It's okay if you don't. I've had enough pissed-off people for one day."

We both laughed.

"Hmm. This could be interesting." I cleared my throat as Paul held my gaze. "I'm here because I needed to get away from home, from everybody that loves me. That sounds weird, huh?"

Paul shrugged and raised his eyebrows.

I grabbed my beer and drained it. "About three months ago, I had a pretty bad accident where I was working. I guess pretty bad is an understatement. It was really bad, actually horrible. One of my best friends died." My stomach tightened. I swallowed.

"Those scars on your feet have something to do with it?" Paul asked.

"Yes… me and my buddy were hit by electricity when we were working. I came out alive, with just those…" I gestured at the scars… "he came out dead." I could hear the waves rolling against the beach and the cry of a few seagulls squabbling nearby in the sand.

"I've been pretty screwed up ever since. I just needed to get away, to move on and get this thing over with. What you said earlier this morning about people who just go with the flow, well, that was me for the first 28 years of my life. But now...now one thing's for sure, there is no flow. I guess I'm looking for someone to tell me what to do, how to get past this."

Paul cleared his throat. "Sorry to hear that, Jake. Seems like we might be kindred spirits down here."

"Yeah, maybe."

"So how long are you stayin'?"

"I'm not sure. I'm not exactly into planning at the moment."

"You know, Jake, I'm a pretty good listener as well as a talker. I can do some listening tonight over dinner if you want to do some talking."

I looked at him, not sure what to do—which was a familiar sensation to me. Then I remembered Marty's words: be open to following where it may lead me. "Sure, Paul," I said. "That would be great."

Shaking hands, we agreed to meet for dinner later.

6

Direction

"There is no way to grow toward perfection than to be willing and patient enough to start over and over again."

—St. Francis de Sales

"Hey, guys. I'm Rachel and I'll be taking care of you tonight. Can I get you a couple of beers or something?"

Looking up from my menu, I found myself staring into the bright blue eyes of our waitress. Her streaked blond hair was pulled back into a ponytail and wonderfully bright teeth filled her smile. She looked to be in her early twenties, wore not a dab of make-up, and was tan except for the unmistakable lighter shape of sunglasses around her eyes.

Paul chuckled. "Easy boy, easy."

"I'm not sure about my stunned friend here but I'd love a pint of Guinness, Rachel. Thanks. Anything for you buddy?"

"Yeah, uh, yeah, I guess I'll have a Guinness, too. Thanks."

"Great, two Guinness coming up." She told us about the specials, and then turned, grabbing an empty glass off the table next to us on the way to the bar.

"Pretty girl, huh?"

"I'll say. Did I look like an absolute idiot when she first came up to the table?"

"Yes, without question." Our laughter felt good. "But I know an even prettier girl. Her name is Samantha and she lives in Utah, in a place called Moab."

"Utah? I doubt I'll ever be out that far west," I said.

"You never know, Jake. You never know."

Rachel came back with our beers. Then Paul said, "I was thinking more about what you told me this afternoon, Jake, and it reminded me of something Abraham Lincoln once said, 'We dare not disregard the lessons of experience.' I think old Abe had it right. He failed at many things—business, politics, he even went bankrupt. And it seems he turned out to be one of the finest leaders this country has ever known. Why? Perhaps it was because he continued to learn, and this learning enabled him to continue to move in the right direction in his life, with the appropriate focus. I see it like this—wrong turns are often needed to get on the right road."

"Hmm, makes sense, but how do I figure out where I want to go… where I want to *be*? A lot of times when I think of what I want to do, I get scared."

"Scared?"

"Oh, yeah, sometimes really scared. I'll get these real negative thoughts in my head, thoughts that tell me I'll never be able to do what I dream of. I always see someone else taking my spot… being the person I wished I was. They got it because they were better than me."

"You do have a choice, you know." Paul straightened his back, his voice firmer.

"A choice?"

"Sure, a choice about where you're headed. What's important is the choice must be made with some direction or focus in mind. It shouldn't be a random choice."

I couldn't meet Paul's gaze. "Yeah, I think I'm in random mode. Maybe coming down here was the wrong thing to do, kind of like a wrong turn."

"You know, Jake, I think maybe you should go out to Utah and meet a friend of mine and that girl I told you about. His name is Brendan."

"Who's Brendan?"

"Brendan is hard to describe. To make money, he advises senior executives, but for a living he helps regular people like you and me figure out how to get from a place we don't want to be to a place that we do want to be."

"That sounds mysterious," I said.

"Yes, I guess it is. But it isn't easy to explain Brendan. I first met him probably fifty years ago when I was in my mid-twenties and he was maybe five or six years younger. It was one summer at a playground in our neighborhood when a bunch of us locals were playing some pick-up basketball games."

I'd thought Paul looked fit, especially now that I knew he was over seventy years old, but I would never have pegged him as a hoops player. "Were you any good at hoops?" I asked.

"I was okay. I had a pretty good jumper but I couldn't dribble that well. Anyhow, I won't go into the details now, but this one night, Brendan defused a near-fight between this kid

Leo and the biggest guy on the court, a teenager named Benny Carrucci, who was a real fighter. Well, Leo and Benny started a shoving match, and Benny was raising his fist, when a hand came from nowhere and grabbed Benny's arm. It was Brendan. He whispers something to Benny, who dropped his raised fist and turns to follow Brendan over to the water fountain."

"So what'd he say to Benny?"

"Great question. You'll have to ask him yourself."

"I can't go to Utah!"

"Why not? You got anything better to do?"

Paul didn't know it, but that was a trick question. "Better," probably not. But I did have something to do that would make a trip to Utah out of the question. Then Marty's voice came to me a third time, be *open to where it may lead you*."

"Uh, I guess not, when I come to think of it." Then I said something without thinking. "Would you come with me?"

Paul's smile was sad. "I don't think now's such a good time for me to make that trip. I have some things that need my focus."

"Oh, hell," I complained. "Come on, Paul. You're trying to talk me into making a crazy trip to Utah. Why won't you come, too?"

I sipped my beer waiting for a reply, then looked at Paul and noticed the tear.

"Hey, what's the matter? I was just kidding. If you don't want to go, that's OK."

"Moab would no doubt be fun, Jake, but I'm afraid I can't go. I need to get some stuff taken out of my body next week back home...some of that nasty stuff." Paul spoke in a calm, slow voice.

"You mean cancer?"

"That would be the stuff." Paul clenched his teeth. "Damn, how this cancer just shows up. I mean I get a checkup every year,

I do my best to stay in shape and eat pretty well, and now this. I need to go back to Ohio, tell my daughters, and head to the hospital to see what the Docs can figure out."

We sat still. The waitress brought our meals, but neither of us said anything for a long time. It was one of those rare times, I remember in my life, when I met someone briefly and felt so connected.

As we finished eating, Paul began to talk again. "You know, I've got a lot racing through my mind, but one thing really excites me—that you need to go spend some time with Brendan. I think perhaps there's something bigger than us at work here. Don't you think it's a little odd how we met?" He smiled and tilted his head.

"One thing Brendan and I love to do is sit in the last moments of sunlight with a cold beer and talk about the 'something bigger than us.' We've had some of the most wonderful discussions. I miss them—and him."

"Don't you think you'll have more? I mean, it'd be great—based on what you've told me about Brendan—if the three of us could have one of those twilight chats. And I'll provide the cold ones." I looked across the table at him. "What do ya think, Paul?"

He looked away and then back, his smile growing larger. "You know, now that I think about it, it's a pretty good idea. It might do me some good. You're on."

"Great." I said. "I need to stop home for a few days to have a couple of conversations. After that, I could shoot right out the Pennsylvania turnpike into Ohio and swing by to pick you up. What do you think?"

"Sounds good to me. I'm going to head home first thing in the morning—I'll catch the sunrise for my soul, a cup of java for the old body here, and then I'll be on the road. I'm going to talk with my daughters and tell them what's going on with me. How about I call you in a couple of days?"

"Sounds good. I hope you can make it out, and I understand why you have to go home."

We finished our dinner and paid the check.

Back in my hotel room I brushed my teeth, did fifty push-ups and hit my knees in prayer, for the first time in many months.

"Dear God, if you had anything to do with my meeting Paul, thanks. And if you didn't, thanks anyway. I know you didn't control what happened with the accident, and I also now know you're here for me. I just want to get better. So please stay around. I'm scared of what I might do. I took a few deep breaths, then finished with a quote I'd always liked. 'Be not afraid of what tomorrow may bring. The same loving God that cared for you today will care for you tomorrow and every day. God will either shield you from suffering, or give you the unfailing strength to bear it. So be at peace and put aside all anxious thoughts and imaginations.'" I paused to reflect on these words of St. Francis de Sales. "I love you."

I climbed into bed, my chest rising and falling with a few breaths, and went to sleep.

I rose early, slipping quickly into my sweat pants and jacket. A smudge of light colored the horizon as I walked barefoot across the cool sand. Paul stood—a silhouette against the deepening orange.

"Good morning."

Paul winked. "Morning to you too. Let's just watch this, and then we'll walk to my car."

There we stood, two human beings connecting with one of the greatest scenes Mother Nature provides. I suddenly realized I was seeing this sunrise differently, my breathing slow, shoulders relaxed, mind still. I made a silent promise to never take another day for granted.

About fifteen minutes passed, the orange faded and the sun blazed as we made our way to Paul's car. He slung his bag into the backseat. "Okay, I'll give you a call in two or three days and let you know what's going on in Ohio. How about you? When are you leaving?"

"I think I'll head out tomorrow. I'm gonna drive down to the Cape Hatteras Lighthouse today. I've got some thinking to do."

"Good deal."

"And, Paul—" I looked intently into his eyes. "—I hope we do chat with Brendan about that 'something bigger than us.'" I swallowed. "I spent some time with God during the accident."

Paul looked at me. "I know. Be well." He climbed into the blue Honda and pulled onto the black road.

I closed my eyes as dust from Paul's tires swept past me and drifted toward the ocean. I breathed deeply, and then stopped by my room.

Minutes later I too was on the two-lane highway, but headed south. The road to the Cape Hatteras Lighthouse lay before me like a runway, not a curve in sight. The lighthouse is a landmark, and a Mecca for East Coast surfers, "Where the waves are big and hollow," is how my brothers and cousins would describe them. As I pulled into the parking lot I couldn't believe that it took a tragedy to get me down here. The lighthouse rose over two-hundred feet in front of me. Its black and white spiral, nicknamed "The Big Barber Pole," was in stark contrast to the blue sky.

I grabbed a beach chair with a big Villanova emblem on it from the back of my truck, and walked toward the ocean. I set my chair on a large, sandy rock and watched the surfers. Thirty minutes later I decided to take a closer look. I walked to the water's edge. The cool water of the Atlantic acted as a salve to my still-aching feet.

Standing calf deep in the clear water I watched a kid of about sixteen drop into a six-foot wave. He turned his board smoothly at the bottom and then steered it straight back up the moving wall of water, hitting the top of the wave just as it was about to break. The young man's rhythmic momentum and the wave's force met perfectly to spin the board around and send him sliding down the face of the wave.

Out farther, another young guy in his twenties hooted loudly as a man with long, gray hair urged him on from a nearby board. The man watched as the surfer popped over the top of the wave toward the open ocean, dropped to his stomach and began paddling back toward his supporters.

I realized that this was a father surfing with his two sons. And for a moment, just an instant, really, I envisioned myself as that older man surfing with my own sons.

And it struck me. This was the first time since the accident that I'd been able to see myself in the future.

I looked back at the father and sons and stood up straight. "If I get through this, as sure as I stand here right now, one day I will surf with my sons," I said out loud. I looked skyward at the seagulls wheeling across the sky, their wings flashing in the sunlight. "You can bet on it."

For the next few hours I lounged in my beach chair, dozing in and out of recurring dreams of hoses, burning smells, and lifeless eyes, leaving me sweating not from the sun, but from terror.

"Villanova!"

My eyes flew open to a man standing there dressed in a white t-shirt and blue shorts. His large, brown-rimmed glasses were covered with clip-on dark lenses, flipped up like an outfielder's.

"You a Villanova fan?"

I nodded, shielding my eyes.

"Sure was a great run in '85 when we won the whole thing. Are you from up north?"

"Yeah." I struggled upright, and wiped the final bit of saliva from the corner of my mouth. I'm from Norristown."

"Norristown!" The man slapped his thighs with both hands. "I'm telling you it is a small world. My name's Hank, Hank Miller. Just down on a short vacation from Jenkintown, not too far from you. Know where that is?"

I reached out and shook his hand. Yes, I knew where it was. It was the town right next to where the accident took place. The man, Hank, was speaking, but I wasn't listening. My stomach ached and dryness came to my mouth as I recalled the smell of my sweaty work boots and socks, mixed with a burnt barbeque scent.

"... so I just thought a few days in a new place was just what I needed."

I shook my head and tried to focus. If anyone could be a poster ad for a grandfather, this guy's it. Besides the clip-on sunglasses, he wore a white t-shirt, gold watch, blue shorts pulled high and white socks, with, of course, black sandals over them. He never stopped smiling, and from the lines on his face it seemed as though he smiled every day for many years.

"So what brings you down here?"

"Oh, pretty much the same as you. Just thought a few days in a new place would do me some good."

"Well, hope you get what you came for. I'm gonna keep movin' on down the beach here. Just wanted to stop to see how you were doing when I saw the Villanova beach chair. Safe travels wherever it is you're heading next." He waved over his shoulder as he turned to walk down the beach.

I stood there, staring at the waves, but not really seeing them. Finally I sat back down.

Just a few hours earlier I'd begun feeling... well, not great, but at least not bad. And now this guy walks out of nowhere and takes me back to the accident and all of the thoughts I'm trying to escape. Why do things like this happen? I looked up to see Hank turning onto a path that led through the dunes. I no sooner turned back toward the waves when I felt suddenly nauseous.

I stood, looking toward where Hank had gone. My eyes followed the smooth sand from where he had been standing in front of me to the point where he'd turned into the dunes. The hair on my body stood and goose bumps appeared as I realized there were no footprints.

I couldn't help but wonder. Was Hank just a vision created by my own mind? Was he an angel? Or maybe it was Brian as he would have looked as an old man if I hadn't killed him, come down to remind me that I can't escape the past.

I hurriedly walked toward the dune trail, squinting at the ground for any trace of Hank and then I began running, ignoring the pain in my feet. I didn't care how much it hurt. Arriving at the trail head, I looked down the path but saw nothing except the surrounding dunes on either side. Hank was nowhere in sight.

7

Homecoming

I tossed and turned in bed that night, waking often. I finally rolled over to see the clock glowing 5:11 and got out of bed. I shoved my clothes into my black duffle bag, left a twenty-dollar tip with a thank you note on the bed for the housekeeping staff and headed for the door. Turning back for a final look, I was glad I hadn't carried out my original plan… though the garden hose was still in the bed of my truck.

I dropped my room key in the black box hanging next to the office door, my thoughts turning to Paul. Wonder if he got home okay? Wonder if he talked with his daughters? Or to the doctors?

My headlights cut the dawn as I pulled onto the highway and headed inland away from the coast. A few miles up the road I stopped to get some gas and a coffee. Back in my truck I began to think about Hank, the mysterious man on the beach. What the heck was that all about? It seemed like a lot of weird things were happening to me lately. I tried unsuccessfully to figure out a sensible answer as the landscape began to change and I passed maple trees and hedgerows. Even the houses became more generic as I moved away from the unique-styled homes of the beach towns. No more houses on pilings with several decks — just vinyl-sided three bedroom homes with two-car garages on half-acre lots. My stomach growled, so I pulled off at the next exit to grab a bite.

After a few more stops, and about 350 miles of highway, farms, cows, and factories, I pulled into my parent's driveway and climbed from my truck. I stretched down to touch my toes and then straightened and reached for the sky, letting out a long breath.

I felt like I'd been gone for an eternity. The brick and white aluminum-sided house that I'd called home for 20 years sat before me in the fading afternoon sun. Memories of the fun and laughs with my family crowded my head like never before. I see my sister in a blue prom gown with her football-player boyfriend who's wearing a light blue tuxedo with a navy velvet bow tie and matching lapels. My Uncle Joe's white Corvette Stingray is parked at the curb, and I'm wishing I was sixteen so I could drive it. Then my brother Bill and I are playing one-on-one and he strips the basketball from my hands, sinking a jumper to beat me yet again in another of our driveway duels. The maple tree in the yard behind the basket is as tall as I am. Then I returned to the present and see the same tree, now three times my height, rising above our chimney. Man, where'd the time go?

Mom ran to me from the front porch. She wore jeans and a light green sweatshirt; her glasses perched atop her brown, shoulder length hair. She smiled broadly. "Well, hi, Jake. You made pretty good time. It's great to have you home." She hugged me as I kissed her cheek, thinking of the moment in the phone booth just days before.

"You're tan," she continued. "You look good. How was your trip? Is it pretty there in the Outer Banks? Mrs. Hay says that it's beautiful this time of year. Meet anybody interesting?"

It's great how some people—my mom at the top of the list—just rattle off questions. She would have been a hell of a detective. But again, having raised seven sons and a daughter, she had a lot of practice.

"The Outer Banks were pretty cool, Mom. I think the beach and the towns down there are how Avalon must've looked fifteen, twenty years ago. It's very natural, no curbs or sidewalks, just simple roads cutting through sand."

"Hey, Jake." My dad walked out from the garage. "Good to see you back. How are the feet? You know you have to get them back into ski boots this year. I'll grab your bags and take them upstairs."

We hugged. "Thanks, Dad." I remembered his tears on the day of the accident. I could count on one hand the times I'd seen my dad cry.

He reached into the back of my truck and grabbed my bag. "Sure. No problem. Hey, what's the hose for? You gonna do some gardening or something? You can water your mothers' mums."

"No, no." I laughed nervously. "That's been in there for a long time. I can't even remember where I got it."

Dad walked into the house as I turned to see my mom studying me. "How are you doing? Really doing?" Her eyes never left mine.

I'd seen this look—it was no use trying to pretend or skirt an issue.

"I feel much better after the trip, Mom. I still have a lot to work out. Those bad thoughts can still invade my mind in an instant...without warning."

"Well, maybe they'll go away soon."

"I dunno. I really hope so. I tried not to, but I did drink a lot the first part of the trip. I was just trying to make the hurt go away, or get drunk enough so that when I woke up everything would be back to normal. I know—now—that isn't gonna happen. I went down there..." I paused and looked away, my bottom lip quivered. "Mom, you want the truth?"

She nodded once.

"I went down there not sure if I was going to come back. But then we talked on the phone that night and you asked me, 'When are you coming home? We can't wait to see you.'" I stopped, unable to speak. I bit my bottom lip and stared past our dead end street at the golf course I'd played so many times.

My mom took my hand. I'm not sure how long we stood there. I heard nothing. Finally, I took a deep breath. "Anyhow, two days ago, the day after our conversation, I woke up ready to get better...or at least to try to begin to move in the direction of 'better.' I did some early morning body surfing and met this really cool old guy named Paul."

I told her about Paul and our conversations about vision and direction and how fast life goes.

"Well, I'm glad that you met a friend—someone to talk with."

"Yeah, he was great."

Just then my younger brother Mark's car pulled into the drive and he hopped out. A few inches shorter than me, he wore jeans, flip-flops and a long-sleeve t-shirt.

"Yo, brother—what's up?" We hugged. "How was your little getaway to the Outer Banks? Waves pretty good?"

"Oh, yeah. I was thinking of you when I went to Hatteras. It was chest to head high."

"Man, sounds nice."

"How's school? You off to a good start?"

He shrugged. "It's alright. But come on, brother, it wasn't long ago when you were there. I'll be okay. It's just a matter of getting back into the swing." His face took on a more serious expression. "So, how are you really, man? Are you feeling any better about all this shit?" He put his arm around our mom. "Sorry, Mom."

"You should be. You know I don't like you and your brothers cursing."

He kissed her forehead and winked at me.

"I guess I feel a little better. It's just really hard."

"You'll get it back, Jake. Just give it time. All my friends ask about you and they say you just have to give it a while. John said it really took him a long time to start feeling okay after his mom died."

"Yeah, I guess. Well, it is good to see you. You gonna be here for dinner?"

"Yep, then I've got to head back to the library to study for a few hours." He slung his backpack over his shoulder and grabbed my arm. "I'm here if you need to talk or anything."

"Thanks."

I grabbed a quick shower, and then enjoyed a great dinner of chicken in a cream sauce with rice and green beans with my mom, dad, Mark, and two of my other brothers, Patrick and Kevin.

Just as we were finishing up the front door swung open and the voice of my sister Terri—my oldest sibling—filled the front hall.

"Hello, everyone. I heard Jake's back. Is that right?" She entered the kitchen, stopping first to kiss my mom, then me. I stood and hugged her. She wore a fashionable burgundy skirt and jacket, cream blouse and black high-heeled shoes.

"How are you? And don't give me any b.s." She stuck her tongue out at my brothers. "Yes, I'm gonna be in your business—all of you—so don't forget it." My mom smiled and Terri gave her a high five.

I told Terri the same story I'd told Mom and the others. Our dinner conversation revolved around my trip and some of the things that happened to them while I was away.

Empty plates sat in front of us by the time Terri and my brothers began excusing themselves one by one. Dad patted my back as he passed me on his way toward his chair in the family room to watch the news. "Really is good to have you back home, son."

I cleared the table as Mom loaded the dishwasher. She had that look on her face I knew too well—deep gaze, lips together, head tilted slightly. Her lips broke into a forced smile that I suspected was not the result of her true thoughts, but rather an attempt to right a wrong.

"Mom, what are you thinking?"

"Here, let's sit a while. I'll get us some tea. You know how much I love to make tea and chat with my kids—you know; find out how they're doing."

"Oh, I know." I pulled in my chair.

Mom dunked her tea bag three times, pulled if from the steaming mug and placed it on her spoon. She then wrapped the string around it, squeezing out the last of the tea. *God, I wonder how many times I've seen her do that.*

Mom looked at me with a more relaxed smile, her hands cupped around her mug. "Jake, I'm going to be really honest. I'm very worried about you. And not just me. Your sister and brothers call me constantly throughout the day to see what's going on. They all say they're trying to help you in any way they can, but you seem to be shutting them out. Before you went to Carolina I was going to talk to you about why you're not going to Mass, but I thought maybe it was just a phase. I know what happened was horrible and that it may take some time to get better, but we don't know how to help."

"Mom." I took a deep breath. She just touched on about 20 things. *Man. What's she talking about, she has no idea how screwed up I am. I'm ready to attack her and defend my behavior, but why? Wait. Take a deep breath. Okay, another, good, now talk.*

"You know, Mom, maybe that's what I really need to deal with—I need to deal with whatever it was that happened that day." I recounted—in vivid detail—what had taken place. "So I guess this is what I struggle with. I'm here and I don't want to be. I have no idea where to go or what to do. A couple of months ago I was ready to move back to Aspen, but I still wasn't sure about my relationship with Lauren. Whether I wanted to be away from her. And now—now—I'm as lost as I've ever been, and alone. Even though you and everyone else want to help me…I feel so alone."

Just then the phone rang and Mom rose to answer it. "Hello." She paused for a brief moment. "Oh. Hello, Joe. Yep, he's back alright. I'll put him on."

I took a deep breath. Joe was, and still is, my best friend. We met in third grade playing football on the golf course with a bunch of other guys. We'd gone to different high schools so we drifted apart. But then years later we shook our heads in disbelief when we found ourselves staring across the room in the same orientation group on our first day at college. Our friendship was quickly renewed and has strengthened over the years. Still, I'd avoided him just as I had everyone else since the accident.

I took the phone from my mom as she placed her hand on my shoulder and I heard the familiar voice.

"Hey, buddy." Joe's voice sounded natural. "What's happening? How was your trip?"

"Hey, Joe. Yeah, my trip was okay. It was good to get away and try to clear my head. I was actually thinking of you one day. I took my truck over to Okracoke Island and sat at an outside bar on the water and enjoyed a really nice cigar."

"Yeah man, that sounds like something I'd like. Hey how about I come by and pick you up? We'll grab a few beers."

"Yeah, that sounds good. I'm just hanging out with my Mom. What are you thinking, about 8 o'clock?"

"Perfect."

"OK, cool, I'll see you then. Thanks." I placed the phone in its cradle.

Mom looked up at me. "You know, Joe's called a lot to talk with me or your dad to see how you're doing. He's a great friend who really cares for you."

"I know. He's gonna come get me to go to Frank's for a few beers. I think it'll be good to get out and see some of the guys. And I promise I'll just have a couple.....really, I don't feel like I need to get drunk tonight."

"Well good. That's a start." Mom smiled. "You know I think you and your brothers drink too much beer anyway."

"Yeah, yeah, yeah." I playfully hugged her. "Mom, there is one more thing I want to tell you. I'm gonna go out to a place called Moab next week. I'll probably stop in Ohio to pick up Paul and then drive out to Utah to see Paul's friend Brendan. It seems that Brendan is a pretty cool guy with a deep outlook on life. He's written a few books and does a lot of work to help people get—and stay—on track."

"Why do you need to go out to Utah with some stranger you just met when you're surrounded by people you know who love you?" Mom rolled her eyes. "Come on, Jake…"

"I know, I know. Listen Mom, I know I'm lucky to have a lot of people who care about me. I can't really explain it, but right now, that's just not enough. Something just felt right about Paul." She stared into my eyes with a very serious look. "It's like I was supposed to meet him, like he can help me get better. I can't really explain it."

"Jake, this sounds crazy."

I bent down to kiss my mom on the cheek, "Don't worry Mom. It'll be okay. I hit bottom in North Carolina and I'm pretty sure now that I want to get better. I really do. I just don't know how, or where to begin. I gotta get a shower before Joe gets here." I paused and gazed at her. "Thanks, Mom. You know I love you." I walked down the hallway and up the stairs, taking them two at a time and leaving my mom at the table, staring into her tea.

8

Lauren

"The unknown is often approached with both anticipation and anxiety."

–Danny Bader

The next evening, I walked up to the door of Lauren's townhouse. Through the window, I could see her sitting on the couch. I knocked. I used to just walk in but ever since we've been "on and off again," I decided I should knock. She looked up, and her eyes looked worried.

She opened the door. "Hi," I said. "Thanks for letting me come over tonight. I really wanted to talk. It's so good to see you."

We hugged like we were hugging for the first time. It felt good to hold her—if even awkwardly—and smell the familiar scent of her hair.

"I hope you're feeling better. Your mom told me she was talking to you when you were in North Carolina. Do you want a beer or something to drink?"

"No thanks, Lauren." I sat on the chair as she settled back onto the couch. I looked at her. She wasn't smiling.

"So, you wanted to talk?"

Part of me wanted to get up and leave, but she probably had the right to be blunt after the way I'd treated her.

"Uh, yeah, Lauren. I need to talk. We need to talk." I looked out the front window at the flickering street light then back to her. "I want you to know I love you and…"

"Jake." Her voice was loud. "Please don't. Not this again. I think my mom and sister were right when they said I shouldn't even let you come over. I'm really sorry about the accident and all that's happened, and the fact that you're mixed up, but I can't take this anymore. You can't continue to tell me we need to move on, then keep calling me and showing up."

I sat silently like a school child being scolded, slouched in the chair with my head hung to my chest.

"I mean we've had some good times, but I'm coming up on thirty and I can't—I won't—allow you to keep hurting me." She began to cry. I jumped up from the chair.

"No. Stay there. I'm okay. I'm okay." She wiped her eyes with a crumpled tissue as I sat back down.

"I mean sometimes I think I'm crazy. I've got a guy who's asked me out and I think I *should* go, I think it would be good if I saw other people. But I can't. I just want you to make up your mind once and for all. You know I love you, but.…" She paused and looked down at her fingers as they twisted a button on her sweater. Then she looked directly into my eyes. "Jake, you have to get yourself together. Not for me, and not even for us. You've got to get yourself together for you. And don't worry about me, I'll be okay. I do love you, Jake, but I don't deserve this yo-yo ride you've been taking me on."

My eyes filled and I moved to sit next to her. I took her hand in mine. "Lauren, you're right, and I'm sorry. I never wanted to hurt you. I'm just screwed up, even more now. I'm gonna try to get better and then maybe we…"

"Jake, are you not hearing me? What do you mean you're gonna try to get better and then we…we what? I take you back and everything's back to normal? I won't Jake, as much as every bone in my body may want to…" she bowed her head, running her fingers through her hair, "I won't."

I looked to the ceiling, and wiped my nose with my hand. "Lauren, I'm gonna go away to meet with a guy to try to get better. The priests and psychiatrists here just didn't work for me. I'm not sure how long I'll be gone. I just wanted to stop and see you, so thanks. I know that sounds trite and I know it's been really hard on you these past months. I'm so sorry. I do love you and want you to be happy. Please believe me."

We hugged, tightly and warmly. Her voice was breathy, barely audible against my ear. "I love you too, Jake. But I just might not be here waiting when you come back."

We parted and looked into one another's eyes for a moment. I leaned in and kissed her cheek "Bye, Lauren."

"Bye."

I closed the front door behind me and glanced in the window to see her lying on the couch, tissue in hand, staring blankly across the room.

9

A Momentary Lapse of Reason

*"Sometimes—in life—wrong turns are
necessary to discover the right road."*

–Danny Bader

Two days later I stood in the garage wearing a white t-shirt,
jeans, and sandals. Even though it was fall and getting cooler, my
feet still hurt and the sandals were much more comfortable than
shoes. I was traveling light. A black CD box from a friend sat on
the front seat of the truck. My friend said he'd put together some
music for my drive, and that there was also a surprise in the box.
On the back seat of my pickup was my duffel bag, backpack, a
bag full of pretzels, some chips, and cookies that my mom had
baked. The hose remained, barely visible under an old tarpaulin
I'd thrown in the back.

I was tossing some trash into the garbage can when Mom came into the garage wearing jeans, a sweatshirt and her slippers. She carried a cup of tea. "You all set?"

"Yeah, Mom. I think I'm good to go, and it looks like the weather's gonna be okay too."

"The weather is supposed to be great." Dad entered the garage from the driveway. "You might hit a little rain as you get close to Pittsburgh, but it shouldn't be too bad. Here's a little something extra in case you need it." He pulled an envelope from his pocket.

"Dad, really, I'm okay."

"I know you are, but take it anyway." He winked. "Hey, if you don't need it, give it back and I'll take it to Atlantic City and try to hit the big one on the slots.

"Thanks, Dad."

"You're welcome son. Be careful, and get yourself straightened out." My dad took a step closer. "What you have to do is get yourself going again. Just use this trip to figure out what you want to do—and then do it." He gave me a kiss on the cheek.

I believe most people have a river of love running through them; it's just that for some that river is farther below the surface. It was really good to feel my Dad's river again.

"I will, Dad. I will." I swallowed. "Okay, guess I better get going."

Mom's look was serious. "You know, you don't have to leave again."

"Yeah, Mom, I do. I'll call you from the road." We hugged and I kissed her. "Don't worry. I'll be fine."

I jumped into my truck, backed out of the garage, and honked twice. In the rearview mirror I saw Mom standing in the driveway, tea cup in one hand, waving with the other. I turned my focus to the road ahead.

I reached into the box and grabbed a CD and slid it into the player. It was a copy of the album, *Momentary Lapse of Reason*. I laughed and said out loud, "Yeah that sounds about right."

The music was enjoyably haunting, the lyrics connecting with my situation.

A soul in tension that's learning to fly
Condition grounded but determined to try

Oh you can say that again, I thought. I'm definitely a soul in tension, and my condition is grounded. That sounds like a bad electricity joke.

Perhaps this is my momentary lapse of reason. Perhaps this is one of those seemingly irrational moments in a person's life—my life— where the action makes sense only to the person taking it. A time when they're absolutely certain they cannot move on without it.

There is a definition of soul I'd seen and committed to memory…the spiritual essence of a man or woman. I liked that it was "spiritual essence" and not "religious essence." I'd always been taught that religion was designed to teach and encourage people to love, but I'd certainly experienced the opposite.

I wonder how many people ever think about the problems they face in this life as connected to their soul. Perhaps that's where people come from who call on their faith to eliminate the tension—to get past their challenges.

Late in the afternoon I pulled my truck to the curb of a maple tree-lined road. Leaves had fallen and the lawns of the houses were turning brown and thin. I pulled the folded piece of paper from my pocket and checked the address against the one on the white mailbox, 1147 Sumpter, I walked up a brick path, the leaves crunching under my sandals, and rang the doorbell. I could hear rustling behind the door and a young voice, "I'll get it!" The door cracked open to a pair of serious, deep, brown eyes.

"Hi. My name's Jake. I'm looking for a man named Paul. I'm a friend of his."

The child glanced back, and turned, studying me. "Hi, Jake. Did you ever read Jack and the Beanstalk? It's my favorite book. Your name is kinda like Jack."

I chuckled. "Yeah, kind of. I read that book a long..."

"Would you be scared if you had to run from the giant?"

"Well, let's see..."

A dark haired woman appeared behind the young girl.

"Hello. May I help you?"

"His name's Jake," said the little girl. "You know, kinda like Jack. He was gonna tell me about running from the giant that lives up the beanstalk."

The woman smiled. "Oh, hi, Jake. Welcome. Dad told me to expect you. Kate, I don't think Poppy's friend is interested in Jack and the Beanstalk right now. I'm Maureen, Paul's daughter. Please come in, and welcome to our house. Dad's in the backyard."

"Thanks, Maureen. Nice to meet you." We shook hands. "But no need to apologize about the Jack thing." I turned to Kate. "Maybe we can talk more about giants later." Maureen reminded me of Paul; she had his eyes, bright blue, and a bit more oval than round. But his energy was missing.

"Sure," Kate said as she skipped ahead of us down the hallway.

I followed Kate and Maureen through the back doorway and we stepped down onto a brick patio surrounded by a low stone wall. Black iron chairs and a table sat next to an outdoor fireplace. Green and white striped cushions sat on the chairs and matched an umbrella spread over the table. An opening in the middle of the wall led to a big yard and one of the largest swing sets I had ever seen. Nets, slides, tubes, and steering wheels hung from wood beams. There were several kids all over, but there, in the tower attached to the end of the structure stood Paul, a young girl at his side. Her thick brown hair hung beneath a black pirate hat.

Paul waved to us. "Ahoy there young lad. What is thy name and what is your business here on these high seas?"

The young girl did her best to mimic his British accent, "Yeah, young lad, what do you want?"

Maureen gave me a sidelong glance. "You never know where you're going to find yourself out here. Lately, we've been on an iceberg in Alaska, stranded on a desert island, and circling the Earth in the space shuttle. One day—my favorite, perhaps—was when we were on a large boat out beyond the breaking waves in Hawaii. We took turns jumping off and surfing giant waves."

"I say again, young lad? What is thy name?"

"I am Jake. Jake of Pennsylvania and I request to come aboard."

"Permission granted. Come aboard."

I climbed up the rung ladder next to the yellow sliding board and stepped onto the deck of the ship.

"Ah, young Jake of Pennsylvania. Good to see you, my boy." Paul leaned over and gave me a hug. I observed the activity on the ship until I was ordered to swab the deck by our three-foot-tall pirate, I was then forced to "walk the plank"—which really meant going down the slide for some juice and cookies.

Paul, the children, and I walked into the large kitchen in the house. We enjoyed our juice and cookies until finally things calmed down and it was just me, Maureen, and Paul at the kitchen table.

"So…" Paul looked at me intently. "Do you want the good news or the bad?"

"I guess the bad."

"Well, the bad news is that I can't go with you to see Brendan. I'm sorry. It would have been a good ride. We could have had some great conversations, a few beers, and gotten you squared away on your vision." Paul stared out the window. "Hmm, I am going to miss that landscape where Brendan lives, you see the most gorgeous and soul-soothing sunsets. And the arches in the national parks are spectacular."

Paul turned toward Maureen as an uncomfortable silence began to grow. The chair creaked as I shifted my weight. "The good news…" He paused and took a deep breath. "The good news is that I'm going to stay here with my family…because I'm dying."

I responded quickly. "Ah, come on, man. That can't be true." I looked at Maureen, tears filling her eyes, then back to Paul. "I mean, I know you said you had to see some doctors, but…" I paused, my voice getting lower. "What do you mean, you're dying?"

"How about a beer?" Paul clapped his hands and folded them on the table.

"Great idea." Maureen wiped her eyes and went to the refrigerator.

She set beers down in front of Paul and me, and settled into her chair.

"I've been alive—well, I use that term 'alive' loosely. Alive? Yeah. Well, my body has been working for a long time, but there have been many days—many wasted days—when I wasn't really alive, I was just living. And to me, now more than ever, there's one hell of a difference between being alive and just living.

"Now, after more than..." Paul looked at Maureen. "What was it that I figured out on the calculator with Kate? Oh yeah, over 27,740 days. After more than 27,740 days on this Earth, I'm now faced with thinking about how many more I have left."

I listened as my untouched beer began to sweat a puddle on the table.

"So here's the deal, Jake. I choose now to be with my family. You know I care about your journey, and Brendan knows this as well. Right now, though, I need to be here. Not because it'll be easier for everyone now, while I am here, but so that it will be easier for everyone when I'm not here. The cancer, or rather, my cancer—I guess I can claim this thing as mine—is strong and far along. My body has done what it can. Now, I do believe in miracles. You know the things that happen in life that just can't be explained by the laws of this world. I think someone has to deeply believe that the miracle will happen. And this is what I call faith, that is, belief without proof. Right now I don't think I believe in a miracle, not sure I'd even want one."

I looked at Maureen. She smiled as if to say "It's okay."

Paul looked at me. "I believe that life's a cycle of transitions. Well Jake, I'm getting ready for life's ultimate transition, and I'll create the other side of this transition, and I'll create it right here, over however much time I'm given. I'll be okay, of this I'm certain. It's the people that are left here afterwards that have the challenge. And remember that they too can create the other side for themselves, or they can just bitch."

Paul pointed a finger at Maureen. "I need to be certain that no one in my family is going to do that when I'm gone."

Maureen laughed. "Okay, Dad, I promise I won't, but I will hurt. And I'm sure I'll hurt pretty badly."

"Well, Mo, hurt is okay, because when you hurt, when someone dies, it means that you loved the person, and their memories are always, always within your soul. So when I think about this, the hurt is love, and love's the greatest energy available to us. So you remember this—your hurt, when I'm gone, is really love, and that is a powerful force." Something in the room shifted when Paul called her Mo.

Mo smiled. "Can this love cry?"

"Absolutely…..absolutely." Paul leaned across the table and kissed her forehead. "Absolutely."

"Good, now I feel a little better."

"Okay, Jake, you go off to see Brendan. I'm thinking that I'll be here on your way back and we can spend some more time together. I look forward to hearing about the growth you'll experience, and what you think about the desert, the river and the canyons. And also about his Jackrabbit. What do you think?"

"Okay, I guess." I looked at Maureen, not sure what Paul meant by jackrabbit. Did Brendan raise rabbits? But I didn't want to worry him with details since he was feeling so bad, and didn't ask. "Hey, Maureen, I'll cry too. I met your dad at a time in my life when I was—and still am—in a big hole. A big, deep, bottomless hole."

Mo gave me a wink.

"Often, actually most of the time since the accident, I can't see a way out of this hole. Spending just a little time with your dad has made me realize—made me hope—there might be a way. Now I just need to find it."

"Not find it, *create* it." Paul gazed into his beer. "The wonderful Irish author George Bernard Shaw once said: *Life is not about finding yourself. Life is about creating yourself.* Jake, you need to go create yourself."

Paul talked on, but I wasn't sure I was fully listening. I was thinking about losing someone else in my life that I cared about. I think he said something about needing to have a vision, a picture of something that's not yet real, and then I think I heard the word action. It was some minutes before I tuned his voice back in and began listening for real.

"The reason I want you to see Brendan," he said, "is that he'll give you other ways of thinking to consider in your life—thinking that can lead to behavior. I believe this thinking and the behavior that comes from it will always allow you to keep moving forward toward your vision, and to recover when things maybe don't go as planned. Brendan will explain this; it's what he simply calls Jackrabbit. It's a simple philosophy that's allowed many people to change." He paused. "Change for the better."

We finished our beers and spent time laughing. Maureen told hysterical stories about her father, particularly the time he slept all night in the hammock dressed as the Easter Bunny.

Before going to bed in the guest room I sat down on the bed and pulled a yellow legal pad from my backpack. I wrote the number 365, then the number 28 below it. I did the math longhand: 10,220. *No way, I've been alive for over 10,220 days.*

I then wrote down another number, 38, and did the math again. 13,870. That was how many days Brian had had on this earth. And because of me, he and his children had probably lost out on at least that many days with him.

I stopped myself from going down that path any farther. *I don't feel too alive right now, more like just living as Paul said. I think Kate was onto something today when she asked me about running from giants. I've had to run from a few in my life and I sure as hell feel like I'm running from a big, nasty one right now.*

10

Population 4,700

*"An uncertain state is an okay place
to be, just not an okay place to stay."*

–Danny Bader

A few days later, bleary-eyed from lack of sleep and from smoking the "surprise" my friend had left in the CD case, I passed a green sign that read Moab 100 miles. I had traveled over 1,800 miles, most of it driven in a silence that was only occasionally broken by my singing along to the radio.

Entering Utah, I felt lousy. My stomach was in knots and my breathing was shallow. My mind replayed the accident over and over again, my internal chatter increasing...*Why am I here?*

What am I looking for? This is crazy. Mom was right, I shouldn't have come here. I haven't found any answers surrounded by people who love me, what makes me think I'll find them in Utah? What should I do when I meet Brendan? And what should I say?

My brow tightened. I clenched my teeth and massaged my temples. As I neared Moab about two hours later, I noticed the intense blue of the sky, and the sprinkling of fledgling green, and the soaring red rock walls standing like giant guardrails along highway 128 and the Colorado River on my right. I was mesmerized by the beauty of the river as I slowed down, smooth as a granite countertop in spots and rough like an old farm road in others. I caught sight of a shadow on the side of a cliff up ahead. Driving closer, I realized the shadow was actually a huge hole several hundred feet up the cliff above the river. It was as if someone took a mammoth ice cream scoop to the rock. The hole was a perfect circle. I pulled onto the sandy shoulder alongside some sagebrush, hearing only the lapping of the river against the shore and a distant cry of a red-tailed hawk, and the occasional car passing by. I wondered how long the hole had been there. What really caused it? I knew my ice cream scoop theory was a little off base. I made a mental note to ask someone about it.

I climbed from the truck and walked toward a huge sandstone slab hanging over the river. I jumped onto the rock, sat down, and leaned back. Immediately, the warmth of the rock moved into my hands. It felt good. I closed my eyes and lay all the way down, clasping my hands behind my head. The rhythm of the river produced a whooshing sound that quickly replaced the stress of driving. My muscles felt heavy and I felt like I was sinking into the rock as if it was a giant magnet and I was made of metal. My mind followed my body as I slipped into a nap.

I awoke when the cool shadow of a passing cloud settled over me. I took a deep breath, stood, and stretched for the sky.

As the shadows of the clouds and canyons shifted around me, I realized how this place—while appearing so barren—was actually providing me energy. I felt refreshed and alert. Gazing up at the sheer rock wall I saw cedar, juniper, and other types of bushes growing out of the rock.

I realized that I was smiling, a rare occurrence these days and I relished my refreshed state. Reaching into my backpack, I grabbed the paper on which Paul had written directions and reviewed them. He had called Brendan to see if it was okay for me to come. I'd called a motel in Moab and booked a room for a week, not sure of how long I'd stay in this place with people I didn't even know. I figured I was about twenty minutes from Sammy's Place, the spot where I was supposed to meet Brendan today. It was now just past noon and the sun raged directly overhead.

I pulled back onto the highway and rolled down the windows. The temperature was in the 70s and the air felt clean as I took deep breaths all the way into my belly. Up ahead I noticed two dots on a cliff. Watching the dots peripherally for about a mile I finally said out loud, "No way. Those dots are people." When the climbers were directly out my side window, I pulled over next to a riverside boulder; the trash can next to my truck had a fast food sack peeking out the top. As I reached for the binoculars in my pack, I noticed the faded gold initials on the black case: F.A.S. for Frederick Aloysius Sprissler, my maternal grandfather, was a mailman and also a true philosopher. He was on the constant lookout for knowledge—how to hit a better golf shot, fix a faucet, hang a lamp, do puzzles with children...and most importantly how to live with joy every day. He was always full of fun, but always putting others first. *I wish I was more like him.*

I lifted my inherited binoculars to my eyes and focused on the climbers, gaining instant access into their world. The higher one was a man who looked to be in his thirties. He reached back into a small sack that hung at the base of his spine, bringing out chalky white hands that stroked the rocks, reading the sandstone like Braille. Below him, attached by a rope, was a woman, also with chalky white hands. I estimated the pair was only about fifty feet off the ground. Focusing above them, I figured they had another 350 to 400 feet to get to the top.

I watched for a few moments, the heat of the sun working its way through my t-shirt into my shoulders and arms. The climbers were in constant communication. I could hear their voices, though unintelligible. I wondered what they were thinking with so much of their climb still ahead of them. Are they excited? Discouraged? Tired? Wishing they'd never even started?

Reluctantly, I got back into the truck because I didn't want to keep Brendan waiting. Two miles up the road I saw a sign for River Road, and made the final turn on this leg of my journey. I shut off the radio, took a deep breath, and attempted to control the not-so-comfortable feeling in my stomach. A sign came into view, made of wood and hanging on a black pole in the corner of the gravel parking lot. The dark block letters read SAMMY'S.

The gravel parking lot had a few vehicles in it, although none were cars. I saw a few trucks, two Jeeps, two motorcycles, and an old, white VW Bus. I backed into a spot and turned off the engine.

The two-story, weathered wood building had a covered porch with a wood plank floor resembling the ones I'd seen in the saloons of old western movies. I half expected to see John Wayne swagger out the front door at any moment. Four large windows, two on each side of the front door, were placed evenly across the front of the building. White curtains hung from black iron rods halfway up from the bottom of the windows. In each window hung several neon beer signs...Coors, Miller Lite, Budweiser, Guinness, and a few I didn't recognize. The Guinness sign reminded me of my time with Paul in Carolina. Two wooden benches made from split logs sat on the porch, still covered with bark in some places. Next to the benches sat large clay pots overflowing with daisies, columbine, and sego lilies. The second floor was accessible by a wooden staircase that ran diagonally up the side of the building to a door next to a window.

My stomach growled and my hands were sweaty. Doubt and uncertainty crept into my mind and my inner voice was just about to start its negative chatter. But before it got going, I caught sight of a dusty blue SUV parked at the far side of Sammy's. It was an older, boxy model, and the head of a black lab poked out of a back window. The dog's tongue was out as he looked at me. I'm not sure dogs can smile, but this one sure looked like he was trying.

A loud noise got my attention and I turned to see a man who had come out the side door of Sammy's, carrying a trash bag. He had on a stained white apron, leading me to think that the door led to the kitchen and that this guy was the cook. He was thin, tan, and wore a navy baseball hat with some kind of white mark on the front. He flipped the bag into the can then turned his face to the sun. With his feet shoulder width apart, he closed his eyes and stood motionless. I watched with curiosity as this statue of a man remained this way for a few minutes. Finally, he took a deep breath, stretched his neck from side to side, and went back into the building.

I wonder what that was all about? I turned my gaze back to the SUV that had first caught my eye. There, on the back was the license plate: JCKRBBT. I'd certainly seen a few Jackrabbits along the highway, but I'd never known someone to have that name on a license plate. Then I remembered that Paul had said something about "Brendan's jackrabbit." *I think I found Brendan. Now I'm curious.*

I strolled across the parking lot feigning a relaxation I did not feel. The aroma of daisies reached my nose. I pulled open the solid wood door and found myself standing directly in front of a long bar with stools lining it. Four raised booths sat along the far wall, the corner one occupied by two men laughing as a waitress stood next to them. Four square tables set with silverware and yellow placemats filled the space between the booths and the bar. Pictures and mirrors hung on every available portion of wall space. At the other end was the same layout, except the corner booth was gone, replaced with an old-style juke-box playing a Patsy Cline song. In the center of the wall behind the bar was a large sign:

All people here create happiness...
some by coming and some by going.

I smiled and committed this one to memory, already getting some understanding of why Paul told me he enjoyed this place.

The men at the bar turned, gave me a quick glance, then all of them went back to their conversations, their food, or the TV—all, that is, except one. He sat at the end of the bar next to the wall. From where he sat he could view the entire bar, tables, booths, and front door. He seemed to like this spot. He wore a baseball hat turned backwards and a ponytail hung from it. A bushy, grey beard flattened against his barrel chest and his muscular shoulders slumped forward. A gold mark on his cap just above his creased brow caught my attention.

He stared at me, not necessarily unfriendly, just a stare. Uncomfortable, I turned toward the bar and made my way toward the other end. No one was behind the bar, and I still felt his stare.

I wonder if that's Brendan. No it can't be. I mean this guy looks like he just came back from a stint in Folsom Prison. He must be riding one of the bikes out front. *No way he's Brendan, no way.*

I grabbed a stool, my stomach growling. I cursed myself for never asking Paul what Brendan looked like or how we'd know one another. All Paul told me was how to get here and the day and time to meet. He said he'd talk with Brendan and everything would be okay. Sometimes it's all in the details.

"Hi, welcome to Sammy's. Can I get you something?"

I raised my head to one of the most stunning women I'd ever seen. I struggled for a response.

She smiled. "Need a drink? Or…" she looked at me closely, probably seeing the wear and tear in my eyes, "maybe food is what you need."

"Uh, yeah, I guess. I mean, uh. What do you…uh… have on draft?"

She turned her head slightly to read the tap handles hanging from the stainless box in the middle of the bar not far from where I sat. "Miller Lite, Guinness, …."

Now that oxygen seemed to have returned to my brain, I realized I could've looked at the handles myself. "Guinness. A Guinness sounds great."

"Comin' right up."

She grabbed a glass, then pulled a handle and let a foamy liquid shoot down into the middle of the glass sitting on the grate until it was half-full. "Let's give that a minute to settle and I'll top it off." I was happy to see she knew how to pour a Guinness.

A moment later, she flipped a coaster onto the bar, sat down the pint, and handed me a menu. "Here you go. I really think you should eat something, too. What about it?"

"Sure, thanks. Just give me a minute with the menu." She moved down the bar and began speaking with the mean-looking dude in the pony tail. I couldn't quite make out all the words, but he kept glancing in my direction. Once he and the bartender caught me staring, and he said something that made her laugh and look in my direction.

I quickly turned my gaze back to the menu. It was hard not to stare at the woman. She was about thirty-five with shoulder length brown hair streaked blond. Her thin face had lines at the sides of her mouth when she smiled, revealing straight and very white teeth below a narrow nose and clear, brown eyes. "Chiclets" is what my Uncle Bill calls nice teeth, and she sure had a pack of them. Her tan skin stood out against a white v-neck t-shirt. She wore jeans and a leather belt with a silver and turquoise buckle.

As I scanned the menu the door opened and a couple entered the restaurant. The man was tall, with brown hair, broad shoulders, and a slight paunch. The woman was shorter, with a lean face and the stride of a gymnast. The woman behind the bar called out to them: "Hey guys. Good ride today?"

"Absolutely, Sammy. Today was great. We spent about four hours riding out near Poison Spider. We're starvin'."

My mind raced back to Paul's comments in the pub that night in North Carolina. I remembered him laughing at my nervousness saying he knew a girl who was prettier than Rachel, the waitress. *Prettier indeed. Absolutely gorgeous is more like it.*

Man, this place is hers? What a cast of characters in here. I got the biker dude over there who looks like he wants to kick my butt, and may even be Brendan, and Sammy—who looks more like she could be on the cover of some fashion magazine. I glanced at her leaning on the bar talking with the couple.

In the corner booth the man facing me was probably in his 40s, with a short military-type haircut. High and tight, was the way my former-Marine dad used to describe it. He wore a white golf shirt and sat as if his spine was a two-by-four. His eyes never left those of the guy sitting across the table from him, who wore a faded denim shirt and a pair of sunglasses sitting atop long, thick grey hair. I watched for a moment until the short-haired man stood, shook hands with the grey-haired man, and left the bar.

"So, any food today?" the bartender asked.

"Sure, that... that would be great. How about the turkey club. Rye toast please."

She jotted down the order.

"So, you're Sammy."

"Excuse me?" She looked up from her notepad.

"Oh, sorry. I guess I was thinking out loud. I said 'So you're Sammy.'"

"Yep, I'm Sammy. Actually Samantha Jane Windermere, but Sammy's just fine. I guess my dad wanted a son." She shrugged.

I searched for a response, something cool that she'd always remember. Nothing.

Sammy tilted her head, looking at me through squinting eyes, her nose scrunching. "You're Jake."

I confirmed her comment as I blinked in surprise.

"You know, I should've figured that when you came in. I've just been so busy and forgot you were coming. I have it on my calendar, but I guess just writing it down isn't good enough." She smirked. "Looking at the darn thing once in a while would help, wouldn't it?"

"How do you know who I am?"

"Well, let me see. There is this friend of mine back in Ohio..." She giggled.

"Paul called you."

"Yep. Paul called the first night after he met you on the beach in North Carolina. He said you'd probably be coming this way."

"How'd he know back then, I wonder."

"I can't say for sure, but Paul just kind of knows stuff about people. Amazes me sometimes. He said then—and I can see it in your..." She stopped and looked away. "Sorry, it's really none of my business."

"What do you mean?"

"Ah, nothing really, I guess. Paul told me something once that I will always remember, and he mentioned it again that night he called." She looked right at me. "He said, 'sometimes we need to make some wrong turns in life to get on the right road.' I sensed that Paul thought you going to the Outer Banks was maybe one of those wrong turns."

I reflected back on the day in the store shopping for a hose, and then meeting Paul. "I can't answer that yet," I said. "All I know right now is Moab sure is a long way from Philly. I hope coming here is a better idea."

"Yeah, me too." She grinned. "I've seen many people come here to visit with Brendan—myself included—and most have left headed in the right direction." Sammy paused for a moment, looked away, and then back. "Or at least a better direction."

"What do you mean 'myself included'?"

She tore the page with my order on it off the pad and turned toward the kitchen. "Oh, nothing really, we'll talk about it later... maybe. Right now, you need to eat."

I lifted my pint and gazed at the bottles on the back bar, thinking about where I was. Yeah, but where's Brendan? Sammy returned from the kitchen and stopped in front of me. "Hey, sorry for not knowing that you were you."

"That's okay. I'm glad I'm here—I think."

The biker guy at the end of the bar was still studying me. I leaned over the bar toward Sammy; she moved in closer.

"Don't turn around, Sammy, but the guy at the end of the bar with tattoos and beard has been looking at me ever since I came in." I leaned back a bit from the bar and paused. "Is he Brendan?"

Sammy looked over my shoulder and smiled.

"No, that would be me," a deep voice said.

I turned and looked into the eyes of the grey haired man from the corner booth. He had tan, weathered skin, light eyes, and the same little smile lines at the corner of his mouth that Sammy had.

"Hello, Jake. Welcome to Moab." Brendan extended his hand and we shook. "I spoke with Paul this morning and he sends his best."

"Hi, Brendan. Nice to meet you finally, and thanks for letting me come out here. How's Paul doing?"

"Oh, you're welcome, and nice to meet you as well. Paul said he's really tired. Not so much from the medication, but more from all the energy he's investing in his family. They're really upset and struggling with this situation, especially a few of the grandkids." Brendan nodded to the barstool next to me. "Mind if I sit?"

"No…no, not at all. You want something to eat?"

"No, thanks. Just had some lunch."

"Yeah. I noticed you over there, didn't even know it was you. I was kind of thinking you… or, rather, Brendan, might be the guy down at the end of the bar."

Brendan glanced down the bar and waved at the biker. "Hello, Preacher. What's going on?"

"All's well, Brendan. I've been meaning to come out and spend some time in the hot tub…if that's okay."

"Anytime you like. You know where the wood is."

"Thanks." He raised his glass to Brendan. "I'll be out soon." Preacher gave me one more look before turning away.

"What's that guy's story? I feel like he wants to come down here and punch me."

"Oh, don't worry about Preacher. He's got a great heart. It's just that he can be a little rough when he doesn't know someone. Maybe he just needs to talk to you."

"Yeah, maybe." I still felt nervous about the guy. "So you have a hot tub? I thought you lived very simply out near some canyon. Paul said it's a very peaceful place."

"And hot tubs aren't simple and peaceful?"

"Well, I've always thought of them as...I don't know, for the rich."

"Maybe you'll want to reserve that judgment until you see my hot tub." He laughed. "So how was the ride out? Ever been out this way before?"

"I've never been this far out west by car, although I flew to LA a few times. I did spend two winters in Aspen several years ago—really liked it there."

Sammy appeared with my sandwich piled high on a black plate. "Here you go, Jake. Need anything else?"

"Nope. I think I'm good. Thanks, Sammy."

Brendan and I chatted about Moab and the surrounding area as I ate. After I finished, I turned to him. "I hope you won't take this the wrong way, Brendan, but Paul didn't really tell me much about you. All he said was that you coach executives to earn money, but for a living you help people get out of places they don't want to be in. So what are you? A psychologist? Motivational speaker? Author? Coach?"

Brendan paused a moment, wearing a grin. "You know, I've been called all of those. And several more, some not so flattering."

"Like what?" I bit down on a large chip.

Brendan thought for a moment then said, "Kook. That's probably one of my favorites. I'm definitely not a psychologist. I mean I don't have a degree, well, a formal degree, though I have studied many people over the past forty or so years. So I guess I have some level of competence on speaking about human behavior. What am I? The label I like the best is 'philosopher.' A young lady from New York, a big shot on Wall Street called me that. We met years ago when she was out here to 'escape' for a few days. That's what she told me then, 'I just needed to escape.' That whole concept of having to 'escape' from life, the life a person chooses, always gets me thinking. A 'break,' or 'time-out,' sure, but an 'escape'? Isn't that what one does from a prison?"

I nodded. "Yeah, I guess so."

"She called me a philosopher because she once read in a book, *The Art of Possibility*, that the ancient philosophers actually saw their job as worthwhile. They believed their purpose was to get people to think about their lives and their world in a way that made them happier and more fulfilled."

Brendan was silent for a moment, gazing at nothing in particular. He spoke softly, more to himself than to me. "Yeah, I like 'philosopher.'"

"Sounds pretty good."

Brendan straightened on his barstool. "We're all philosophers to some degree."

"We are? How? Just by getting people to think?"

"Sure. People—me included—need to think more. See, what we think is the basis for our action. Emerson once said, 'The ancestor of every action is a thought.'"

"I like that." I swigged my Guinness, then pushed my plate away. I was silent as I looked into the mirror behind the bar and saw myself staring back. Brendan rotated his soda bottle. He seemed comfortable with the silence.

I fidgeted, and thought for a minute before asking my question. "So, do you think you can help me?"

He looked up to the corner of the ceiling, then turned back to me. "That depends."

"On what?"

"On how you answer one question."

"What's the question?"

"Why are you here?" Brendan pursed his lips and raised his brows as if to encourage a response.

I looked back at the mirror, thought for a moment, and repeated the question in my head. Good question. *Why am I here?*

I thought back to what had happened and its impact on others. It had rocked me into this brutal tailspin....a time of grief, guilt, fear and despair. *Had I come here to stop drinking? To seek forgiveness? To make the nightmares stop? Had I come to convince myself that I was not to blame? Had I come to continue running? Was I still running, or had I come to a stop?*

My head dropped. "Tough question, Brendan, it feels kind of weird telling you about stuff when I don't even know you. I think I may need another Guinness before I can answer it."

Brendan responded. "As you like, but I haven't seen the most valid answers come from that approach."

I didn't say anything for a while, the memories and experiences of the past few months crowding into my brain. I felt tears welling up in my eyes and was embarrassed. *What kind of man cries in front of a stranger?* Then I thought screw it, and turned back to Brendan. "I'm here because I'm messed up. I'm here because things are not good for some people, and I'm not sure

I'm not the one to blame. I'm here because I drink too much, too often. I was a good person all of my life, a good Catholic. And now I hurt people I love and I don't go to church anymore and I think God is full of crap to have let this happen." Tears slid down my face as my voice lowered. "I'm here because I don't know what to do about my on-and-off girlfriend of six years. I'm here because I avoid my Mom and Dad, my best friends, my only sister and my six brothers when they try to talk to me. I'm here because I lie awake in bed at night not sure of what to do the next day. And when I finally fall asleep, the only dreams I have are nightmares. And sometimes … a lot of times lately… I think that maybe it would be best if I went to sleep and never woke up."

I wiped my eyes with the napkin. I was glad there were only a few other people in the bar at this hour. I knew they were staring at me but I didn't care. I took a deep breath through my nose and let it out through my mouth. I took a swig of my Guinness, and looked back up at Brendan. "But then my mom…" I swallowed hard, "my mom told me when I was in North Carolina that she loved me and couldn't wait to see me again. And then I met Paul… and he gave me hope. Not much hope. But a little glimmer that maybe checking out wasn't the right thing to do. So I came here because I want to feel better. I'm really trying to hold onto wanting to be alive again, not just living."

The silence that followed was brief as Brendan placed his hand on my shoulder. "Good. Great answer." He smiled. "I can't help you."

I blanched.

"But," he continued slowly, "I'm certain that your time out here in the desert will allow you to help yourself."

I nodded, but didn't feel any relief. "Helping myself is what I've been trying to do, Brendan. And all I did was screw things up even worse. So, you'll pardon me if that doesn't sound like such a great option at the moment."

I drained my Guinness. Brendan sat quietly, nodding at a man on his way to the jukebox. Through a crack in the swinging door I could see Sammy watching from the kitchen. She turned and grabbed a burger from under the heat lamp and walked over to set it at the man's place. She came over to us. "How we doing, guys? Need anything?"

Brendan winked and held her gaze. "Just the check, Sam."

I straightened and reached into the pocket of my jeans, forcing a smile. Sammy placed a hand on each of our hands. "No check today, gentlemen. It's on me."

"You don't have to..."

"It's my pleasure, Jake."

"Thanks, a lot. Hope I can come back."

She cleared the plate and silverware in front of me and looked up. "You will."

"See ya, Sammy. Thanks." Brendan rose from the barstool and turned toward the door. "Let's continue this conversation outside, okay, Jake?"

I followed him out the door.

Brendan went over to the SUV with the black lab, scratched the dog's head through the open window, and then turned to lean against the SUV as he faced me. "I understand what you're feeling, Jake. I know you don't know me well enough to take that at face value yet, but trust me. I've been where you are now. And when I say that you can help yourself, I mean that only you can find answers that fit your life. What I can do is help you find your own answers. How does that sound?"

I realized I'd been hoping for something more profound from this mysterious figure I'd driven so far to meet. But I was too tired to push the point. All I said was, "I'm willing to try just about anything that doesn't involve vodka, drugs, or garden hoses," I said.

Brendan laughed. "I know you don't really mean that as a joke, but it's a great start that you can make fun of your situation. I've got to go now, Jake, but you're welcome to come with me and stay in my bunkhouse if you want. We can talk tomorrow and figure out if and how we might work together."

There's no way I'm staying with anybody out here I thought to myself. "Thanks, Brendan, but I have a motel in town booked, so I'll just stay there." We made plans for me to meet him at his place in the morning.

As he got into his SUV, I asked him if he raised rabbits. He looked at me quizzically. "Rabbits?" he said.

I pointed towards the back of his car. "Yeah, your license plate says jackrabbit, doesn't it? And Paul said I needed to learn about Brendan's jackrabbit."

Brendan chuckled. "Oh, that. Yes, jackrabbits are very important to me, but not for the reason you think. We'll talk about it tomorrow." He nodded at me, then started his truck and drove off.

I got into my truck and drove west towards the hotel. I stopped at a liquor store along the way and stocked up on beer, and a little pleased that I had been able to resist the vodka. *A start, indeed.*

The small motel on the edge of this small town was single story, with fading paint. It reminded me eerily of the motel in the Outer Banks, wooden porch railing and all. My room was very similar as well, and it made my skin crawl. I watched some TV, drank some beers, and fell asleep until the dream woke me yet again.

11

Vision vs. Reality

"As a man thinketh, so is he."

–Proverbs 23:7

Early the next morning I drove out of town, made a final turn onto a dirt road, drove about a quarter of a mile, then saw Brendan's house. He was sitting in a rocker on the front porch. His glasses were perched on his head, the black lab lying by his feet. He raised his mug in acknowledgment as I pulled up and got out of the truck.

"Good morning. How'd you sleep?"

"So-so."

"Hmm." Brendan peered over the rim of his coffee mug. "Want some coffee? The pot's inside. And say hi to Canyon here."

"Sure. Sounds great." I reached down and patted the dog as I walked past him into the house.

I filled a mug from the cast iron coffeepot in the kitchen, added cream and sugar, and returned, taking a seat on the railing.

"So? Not such a good night's rest?"

I shook my head. "No. I had this dream that gets me all worked up."

"Do you have this dream often?"

"Off and on. I was hoping being in a new environment would make it go away."

He paused a moment, then took a sip of his coffee. "Maybe it still will, Jake. But sometimes these things take time. Jake, I know a fair amount about what's going on with you. Besides what you told me at Sammy's yesterday, Paul filled me in on what happened to you a few months back. I hope you're okay with that."

"Yeah, sure. I figured he'd tell you at least a little of what happened."

"How would you describe your state of mind now?" asked Brendan.

"I'm sick of feeling like this. Every day I wake up and try not to feel like crap."

"Then maybe you should try shifting your focus."

"What do you mean?"

"Well, we—as people—usually get what we're focused on."

"What do you mean by focus?"

"Great question." Brendan sat up straighter in the chair, balancing his mug in his leg. "What does focus mean to you?"

I shrugged. "I guess for me it kind of means what you're thinking about."

"Well, yes, sort of. The formal definition someone told me once was the concentration of attention or energy on an object or thing." I nodded my agreement. "Jake, there's a strong connection between what we get out of our lives, what we create, and what we focus on—some people call it the focus we hold. Here's a simple example. Back in 1978, Karl Wallenda, the world famous tightrope walker, lost his balance and fell to his death—he was 73, I think—while attempting a walk between two high-rise beachfront hotels in San Juan, Puerto Rico. Did you ever hear about him?"

"Yeah, the Flying Wallendas, right?"

"Yes, that's the family."

"Maybe not the best example about focus."

"On the contrary, Jake, it's a great story about focus. It seems that Karl's widow and others who were close to him noticed that leading up to his walk he began to focus more on not falling, versus his usual goal of simply— or not so simply — walking across the rope. Have you ever focused so much on something you wanted to avoid, only to have that exact thing happen?"

"But aren't they the same thing said in different ways? I mean Wallenda could either walk across or not fall—either way, mission accomplished."

Brendan paused for a moment, studying me. "Not to me. On that last walk Wallenda was focused alright, but those around him think it was on the wrong thing, on not falling. And he paid a hefty price for having the wrong focus."

I nodded; still not sure I understood his point.

"So, I'm curious. What would you say you're focused on?"

I thought of giving the safe answer that "I wasn't sure," but then I thought more deeply and honestly. "My focus is summed up in four thoughts…first, this all sucks, big time… second, I wonder why I'm here —meaning on this Earth, not here in Moab, third, anger about the people whose lives were changed forever because of a stupid accident… and fourth, how can I make the pain go away.

"And what has this focus produced?"

It didn't take long for me to respond. I merely described my current state of existence. "Pain, alcoholic black outs, drugs, helpless guilt, unintended harm to those around me, I could go on."

There was silence as Brendan continued to rub Canyon's head. I was startled how quickly I'd answered. I thought about how I was here in this unfamiliar place, several months after the accident and how I hadn't really put everything I'd been feeling into words before.

"That's the truth. It's the reality of my situation." I sounded like a criminal squirming under the visage of a stern judge. "So many times I've been accused of living in a dream world. My mom and dad, brothers and sister, even my friends used to laugh and say how removed I was from reality. But now, when I face the reality of my situation… I get the sense that…"

"That what?" His tone was neutral.

"That I shouldn't be. And I don't get it. I don't think I can just shift my focus off of everything that is real for me."

Brendan smiled slightly. "Jake, many people think *shifting* your focus or optimism, or positive thinking, or visualization, or whatever you want to call it—is based on avoiding reality. To me it's quite the opposite. It's being acutely aware of the reality and then seeing what it would look like if it were different, seeing it in another way. You're probably starting to enter that stage now, since you got off your butt and came out here." He winked.

"Yeah, how to get off my butt? The eternal question." I shook my head.

"Figuratively and literally in your case, I guess."

"Trust me, you got that right."

"Here's the point. When you're focused on reality, you're just that, you are concentrating on the here and the now, whatever your situation."

He rose; flipping what little coffee was left in his mug over the railing, and walked off the porch, moving his head for me to follow. He stopped after a few steps and turned to me. "Jake, I asked you to come here this morning to see if we are going to work together. Can we get that figured out?"

"Yeah, sure. How long do people stay here and work with you? And how much do you charge?"

Brendan glanced to the clear sky, then back to me. "You can stay here as long as you'd like. Some people work with me for a few hours and then leave—for whatever reason. Some folks stay around longer. You'll know. As for money, don't worry about paying me."

"No, I'll pay you. I mean I don't want—"

Brendan interrupted. "Jake, Jake. I don't do this for profit. So just say thanks."

"Okay, thanks… and I mean it."

"Alright then, let's get started." Brendan knelt down. "Here, let me show you something. Using the long end of his coffee spoon he began to draw in the dirt. He drew four curved arrows that formed a loose circle, but that were unconnected. In the middle of this he drew a straight line with an arrow on both sides. On the left-hand side of the two-sided arrow, he wrote *"develop vision."*

I knelt down next to him as he continued. "This," the end of his spoon pointing at the words in the dirt, "is where a person may want to spend some time when their focus—as you suggested a minute ago—is not producing the reality they want. You said you continue to feel like crap. When somebody's at a place in their life that's different from what they want, they should spend some time developing vision, or a dream of what they do want.

"Think of this like viewing the coming attractions of their life. It could relate to a relationship in which they're involved, a job, a living arrangement, their spiritual state, or their financial state—simply anything that they want to be different. It's only when one gets real clear on where they want to go, what it will look like when things are different, that they can begin moving in that direction."

"I think I see what you're suggesting. If I think about a better...whatever, it'll happen. Sounds pretty simple to me."

"Sure does, but the thinking is just the beginning. Trust me here, Jake. I've imagined many things in my life—mostly when I was younger—that never became a reality because I wasn't doing anything to make them happen. The other side of this little equation requires effort, activity, perhaps what we may call 'physical focus.'"

He took his spoon again and wrote, this time on the right side of the two-sided arrow. It said "create reality."

"Once we get clear on the vision, then we need to understand and identify what needs to happen, what actions we need to take to get there, to the new reality. This, Jake..." He pointed at the arrow in the middle "this two-way street between developing a vision and taking action is where many people fail. They develop their vision, but they don't identify or execute the action necessary to transform the vision into reality. This is action, plain and simple. And not much is achieved without it. I once heard someone say, 'I don't know if action brings happiness, but I've not seen a lot of happiness without action.' I have, however, seen many people who run around immersed in a world of constant action, of doing, but they don't have..." Brendan moved the spoon slightly back to the left "...the vision. For an action to be truly effective, it must be directed toward a clear vision."

I nodded. "Maybe not so simple. So what you're telling me is, in order for me to get better and get my life back on track, I need to create a vision of how my life will look when it no longer sucks, and the confusion and anger are gone."

"Well, sort of. First, I'm not really telling you this. I've found that telling is not the best approach to support someone who wants to change. I'm merely stating what I've experienced myself and also seen work with many people at a place in their lives not unlike yours. They can often begin to adjust to the reality of today by developing a strong vision of tomorrow."

He stood up and looked down at the drawing in the sand. "Like I said, the vision is really just the coming attractions for your life, kind of like a movie clip for what's coming next. Second, if you choose to develop a vision, I strongly encourage you to leave words like 'sucks,' 'confusion' and 'anger' behind and replace them with their opposites." He paused. "Unless that's really what you want."

"You mean like..." I struggled to find the words.

"Not as easy as you think, huh?"

"No, hold on. I can get it." I concentrated for what felt like minutes but was probably a few seconds. "You mean like fulfilling... contented... and peaceful?"

"Sounds like a good start to me."

"But it's just words, Brendan. Sure I feel better talking about fulfillment than talking about anger. But don't you think

I've wanted those things for a long time? Do you think I wanted to end up with pain and guilt? I'd trade in confusion for contentment right now. But contentment isn't my reality."

"But that's the point, Jake. You can't get out of your current reality until you start believing that something better... a vision of a better reality... is possible. Those words—fulfilling, contented, peaceful–are already real for you when you acknowledge that that's what you want in your life."

I looked back at the dust drawing. "What are the spaces between the arrows? Why are there four of them?"

"We'll continue later, but not right now. Right now I need to go visit a friend. Want to come along?"

12

Jackrabbit

"One's purpose in life is like a compass,
always pointing in the right direction."

–Danny Bader

Brendan and I got into his SUV and made our way down the dirt road that led to the highway. Driving along, I was again aware how peaceful the desert was and how my mind was beginning to relax.

I turned to Brendan. "So where are we headed?"

"Just down the road a bit. I have someone that I want you to meet. I think you'll like him."

I jumped at what sounded like an explosion firing outside Brendan's driver's-side window. I leaned over to see a bright yellow Lamborghini hugging the road right next to the truck, racing its engine. The driver looked at us stone-faced, then dropped the car back into gear, and took off like a shot.

"What a jerk," I said. "I hate it when people with money think they're better than the rest of us. Who cares what kind of car someone drives, or how much money they have. I mean, look at that jerk. Someone could get hurt with him driving like that."

Brendan glanced at me. "Hmm."

"What? You don't agree?"

"Well, since you asked, I have two thoughts on this." He never looked over. "Number one, it's interesting to me that your entire mood and disposition just changed. You and I had a conversation back at the ranch not long ago that seemed to inspire you a bit. And now, that fast"—he snapped his fingers—"you're pissed off at some guy in a fancy car—that you don't even know—who sped by us.

"Number two, I don't think rich people and their money are either good or bad. What is good or bad is the process by which they achieve their material wealth. Are they honest, ethical, and caring? These are the types of things that get my attention. Do they sacrifice their role as dad, or mom, as brother, sister, son or daughter, for the pursuit of a material world? 'Many men can make a fortune, but few can make a family.' I like that quote. I also like to observe what people do with their money. Perhaps it's no business of mine, but I've seen many folks do wonderful things with money. Helping others to get to a better place in life and overcome challenges—now that to me is a good use of money. I also know many people who don't have the financial means to help others. But they have time and energy, and they do wonderful work by their volunteering. Giving in any form is just a good thing."

Brendan turned to me. "Think about this, Jake. You have the opportunity—the choice, today, and every day—to create your own reality and emotions, rather than letting someone else create it for you. Test it out, Jake. When you do, I'll bet you have better days."

I heard Brendan and got what he was saying, but I still wasn't good with it. "So not even a small part of you thinks that guy's a jerk?"

"Nope. Not really." He chuckled as he glanced out the window, rubbing his chin. "But my dad, on the other hand, would agree with you if he was here. He just never seemed to get comfortable with a lot of things, so the result was that a lot of other people—what they said, and did—pissed him off. Oh, well. Anyway, the place where we're heading is a result of what I just mentioned."

"What? Creating reality?"

"Yes. Some of that, and a whole bunch of giving."

The SUV slowed down and turned onto a lane lined with white daisies, yellow marigolds, and all kinds of pink flowers whose names I didn't know. Further ahead were red, blue, purple ones, some more pink ones and some with orange petals and black centers. We approached the first and largest of three buildings sitting in a semicircle at the end of the road. Sunlight lit the red tile roofs. Adobe walls, cedar beams, stained-glass windows and large plates of glass blended in a beautiful building. I slumped as my gaze was drawn to the bright yellow car parked at the corner of the lot.

Brendan gave me a knowing look.

"What is this place? Some type of business?"

My question was partially answered when I noticed a young woman dressed in bright purple hospital scrubs sitting in a wooden chair on a small stone patio to the right of the front entrance. A young boy in a wheelchair sat next to her, waving to us.

I read the simple, silver block letters on the building out loud: "Tuscany Wellness Center for Kids."

We parked and began walking toward the entrance of the building as a man exited toward us. He was a big man with broad shoulders and thick salt-and-pepper hair, combed straight back. He wore black loafers, expensive looking tan slacks and a pressed white shirt, a little tighter across his belly. He walked to Brendan and gave him a burly hug.

Brendan turned to me. "Jake, I'd like you to meet someone."

I looked sheepishly into the man's eyes, having realized he was the driver of the yellow sports car. "I'd like you to say hello to Benny Carrucci. Benny, this is Jake, the young man I told you about last week."

"Nice to meet you, Mr. Carrucci." His grip was firm and his hand rough.

"Nice to meet you, Jake. And please, call me Benny."

My mind raced as the man's name sounded familiar. "Wait a minute. Benny Carrucci...Benny Carrucci. Are you the same— you have to be—you're the Benny Carrucci that Paul told me about from the playground. You're the tough teenager who used to beat everybody up. Wow, here you are. After how many years? When was it that Brendan talked you out of hammering that guy after you lost a game?"

Benny had a broad, natural smile. He shook his head at Brendan. "What have you been telling this guy? Man, you might think I was some type of thug."

Brendan smiled back at him. "Well Benny, I must admit, if there were thugs on the playground back then—and there were—you would have been in the running."

Benny grabbed Brendan and put him in a headlock. "And don't you forget it, my friend. I can easily revert back in a New York minute."

Just then the boy in the wheelchair cleared his throat. "And what about me, you old decrepit dudes? Either of you want a piece of me?"

Benny released Brendan and we all turned to look at the boy in the wheelchair. He'd rolled up to us on his own, the woman in purple scrubs close behind.

"Not me." Benny held out his hand to receive a slap from the boy.

"Good choice." The boy turned to Brendan. "And what about you? Got anything?"

"Absolutely not. You're way out of my league."

"Another smart choice. Okay, now that we've got that settled, who's this joker?"

The young boy in the wheelchair gave a slight nod in my direction, no eye contact, just a nod. He was no more than ten years old, and wore green hospital pants and a white t-shirt. A dark sticker with white letters stuck to the side of his wheelchair: *Caution: This wheelchair has been known to run people over.*

"Well, Noah, this is a friend of mine from Philadelphia. He's here to visit for a while." Brendan turned to me. "Jake, I'd like you to meet Noah. Noah, Jake."

I reached down and we shook. "Nice to meet you, Noah. And based on what I've already seen, I don't want a piece of you, either."

"Cool." His eyes lit up. He turned back to the two older men. "Hey, did you guys tell him about me?"

Both men spoke in unison. "Nope."

"Good." Then he smiled.

Next I was introduced to the nurse in the scrubs. She was tall, dark eyes set between brown bangs and a crooked smile. On her wrist was a black and yellow diver's watch. It seems that she was Noah's personal nurse when she was working—which seemed to be quite often from the conversation she was having with Brendan and Benny.

We made small talk and exchanged goodbyes as the nurse wheeled Noah down a walkway toward a vine-covered courtyard, the faint sound of splashing water from a fountain in the center filling the air. Black iron and wooden benches were scattered around it.

"Come on. Let's get some coffee and something to eat. I'm starving." Benny led us through the hallways, speaking with everyone he passed, some more than others. Brendan brought up the rear, equally chatty.

We arrived at the cafeteria, which felt more like a restaurant. The walls were heavily textured in light brownish-orange with rough cedar trim. A wall of windows stood on the far side, beyond black granite tables with wicker and leather chairs. The place could have easily made the "hot new restaurants in Philly" list.

After loading an array of soups, salads, and sandwiches on our trays, we sat at a table next to the window wall. I turned to Brendan. "So who's this kid Noah? Is he really sick? And what is this place?"

"Yeah, Noah's sick alright." Brendan chewed thoughtfully. "This place is the result of a vision that old Benny here had a long time ago." I looked to Benny who nodded humbly. "This is a place sick kids come to on their road to recovery, to wellness. It's the result of a foundation that's funded solely by Benny."

"Not just by me." Benny wiped his mouth. "But also by my companies, and the wonderful and generous people who work there. They also contribute to make this possible. Some give money. Some give their time and energy, some both."

I nodded slowly, thinking about what it costs to run a place like this. I came up with the answer; a lot. "And what about these kids? Do they all get better?"

"Some do." Brendan took a sip of his iced tea.

"What about Noah? Will he get better? He certainly is a rambunctious little guy."

"Yes, he's a free spirit. We're not sure about Noah just yet. He has a rare blood disease that was diagnosed about a year ago. Up until then he was a normal, healthy kid. He has a brother and sister, and a great mom and dad, and he was just growing up in a small town in North Carolina. He received treatment down there and now he's here so we can focus on getting him well. It's easier for him—and his family—if he's here."

"Wouldn't it be better for Noah and them if they were all together? I mean, so they could see one another, talk with one another?"

"Well, they do actually see one another quite a bit. You see, Benny flies them out, as well as a few of his friends."

"For free?"

"Yes, for free. Benny and some of his friends who own jets donate the air travel. We call them the foundation jets. And when they're not here, several rooms on-site are equipped with state-of-the-art video conferencing equipment where the kids can talk with—and see—their friends and families."

I shook my head and turned to Benny. "Unbelievable."

He sat there grinning at me. We toured the rest of the facility where I saw the patients' rooms, spacious and very comfortable. Brightly colored quilts and pillows were spread over cedar framed furniture. Ansel Adams photographs, in the unmistakable black and white style, hung on the walls. There was a game room, several kitchens and many common areas scattered throughout the building. The physical therapy room looked more like a high school gym and weight room. Banners hung from the walls—Spartans, Bears, Knights, Bulldogs, and many more. Brendan told me they were from the kids' school mascots.

After the tour, we climbed back into Brendan's SUV.

"So why'd you take me there?" I asked.

Brendan flipped on his wipers as it started to sprinkle on our way back home. "Just wanted you to meet Benny and Noah, and see the place. I'd sure appreciate if you could help out there at the center. Maybe do some painting or landscaping—those types of jobs. You okay with that?"

"Absolutely, it would be a privilege." I turned my head to stare out at a mesa in the distance.

When we got back to Brendan's place he asked if I'd like to take a look around. I passed, telling him I was going to head into town.

"Okay, but before you leave I want to give you a peek into tomorrow."

I followed Brendan into the house and took a seat on the end of the couch as he settled into the chair next to me. He held a plain white artist's pad, about 8 by 10 inches, and a purple felt-tip marker. He held it out to me. "Do you remember the diagram I drew in the dirt?"

"Sure, the circular one you did out front here? The one with the vision thing in the middle?"

"Yeah, the vision thing," he said without a trace of irony. "What do you remember about that?"

I scrunched my nose. "Sorry, Brendan. I can't remember the whole thing."

"That's okay. Here, take this pad and draw the circular diagram with the four arrows." He watched. "Good. Now place a two-sided arrow in the middle."

I did so quickly. "Yeah, I remember this. And on the left side was the vision thing."

Brendan smiled, "Develop vision to be exact."

"Yeah, sorry. I guess I'm kind of trashing your model here."

"It's okay. This is just the visual to get people thinking, a guide for them. On the right-hand side you'll probably remember I drew the words create—"

"Reality." I interrupted. "Create Reality. And the arrow here is the link; it's all about the action we take to move from point A to point B, from our vision to our reality."

"Yes, that's it, the first principle you've learned about. Good memory. Now tomorrow, you're going to meet Vanessa. Vanessa works—no, really she volunteers—at the wellness center. You'll spend time with her and she'll talk to you about another principle that people imbed into their lives when they understand Jackrabbit. Everybody has a philosophy that guides them. Jackrabbit is what I call the one that works for me.

I began to hand the paper back to Brendan. "Why do you call it Jackrabbit?"

"A common question. It's really quite simple. When I was developing this model, this approach to living, I wanted to have an animal as the logo for my company and to be a sign for this model, something simple that people would recognize so they stay conscious of what it means to them."

"Kind of like the swoosh?"

"I guess. Anyhow, I researched all types of animals and narrowed it down to a few. The jackrabbit was not even on the list. In the final selection process I focused on one word that's vital to me—vision. I thought about a few, but none of the ones I'd selected really felt right. So, I researched animals and the word vision."

"And the jackrabbit showed up?"

"Yes, and the jackrabbit showed up. An article I read said the jackrabbit has some of the best vision in the animal kingdom because its eyes sit very high on the sides of its head and more toward the back, giving it the ability to essentially see three-hundred-and-sixty degrees—to be aware of its whole environment. For me this was it, this was what I was trying to understand myself, and what I wanted to support others in learning...that to live a happy and fulfilling life we should develop the innate sense to pay attention to all of our surroundings—self, health, relationships, career, family, spirit, money...everything."

"I see, but it sounds so exhausting, keeping track of all that stuff."

"Or like being fully engaged with life?" He challenged.

"Yeah, that too."

Again, I began to hand the paper to Brendan, but he shook his head. "No, you hold onto that. You'll complete it, or maybe we'll complete it later. There are four more principles in addition to develop vision and create reality. So, get a good night's rest and tomorrow morning come over at seven-thirty. I'll drop you at Tuscany. Sound like a plan?"

"Sure does, Brendan." I paused. "And thanks. Thanks a lot."

"You're welcome. Sleep well."

When I got back to the motel I sat down and pulled the top of the marker off with my teeth, leaving it sticking out of my mouth like the end of a cheap cigar. On the top of the paper in the middle I wrote Jackrabbit.

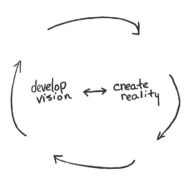

I tore the page off of the pad carefully, folded it in half, then again and put it into the back pocket of my jeans.

I thought about the phone call with my mom back in the Outer Banks, and how—perhaps—after that call I first got some sense of vision, some conception about what it would be like when I got better. I thought about the man and his sons surfing at the beach and how I'd realized I wanted that kind of life someday. But as I drifted off to sleep, I knew that I couldn't actually put myself in that picture yet.

13

Be Still

"It's often in the absence of
sound that we hear the most."

–Danny Bader

I woke slowly the next morning, peering with one eye at the clock as I became more conscious. It glowed 6:27 and I realized the last time I'd checked it was 9:38. I relished the feeling of being calm and relaxed. No racing pulse. No sweaty brow. Wow, I could get used to sleeping like this.

I hit the bathroom, pulled on a pair of jeans and a t-shirt and walked outside. Breakfast was a quick plate of eggs at a diner around the corner, and then I drove out to Brendan's.

Again he was on the front porch when I arrived. "Good morning, Jake. How was your night?"

"Pretty good. I slept the night through."

"Great to hear. Let me just run inside for a minute and we'll get going over to Tuscany."

As we pulled into the drive at Tuscany, Brendan pointed out Sammy's Jeep.

"Sammy's going to work with you today. There's an old storage room—pretty large actually—that we're converting into a place where people can go to find some peace. Some silence."

"Like a chapel?"

"To some, yes. To others, it will be just a place to go." We climbed from the SUV and walked toward the front door and the two landscapers doing some trimming off to the side.

"Will Vanessa be helping us paint?"

"Nope, but you'll connect with her for sure. I'll be curious to hear your thoughts later. Sammy said she'll give you a ride to her place at the end of the day. I'll meet you there and we can have some dinner. She's inside waiting for you." Brendan greeted the two men as we passed, and they stopped clipping long enough to turn and wave at us.

Through the front doors I could see Sammy sitting on one of the yellow chairs. She stood and put her arms out and gave me a hug, catching me a bit off guard as I stumbled.

"Sorry." She laughed as we separated. "I'm a hugger."

"Oh, that's...that's okay." I could feel the warmth rushing to my face.

I looked at her paint-speckled jeans, old grey t-shirt and the brown bandana she wore on her head. "Well, you sure look like you're ready for this painting thing today." Brendan said goodbye to us and was off to some meeting.

"Oh yeah, from the looks of these clothes you can tell I've done this before. We've had to do a lot of painting around here the past few months. It's nice what a fresh coat of paint can do. I paint the rooms in my place every two years—you know, to keep it fresh. I do two or three each year so I don't have to do them all at once—that would probably never happen." Sammy flipped her head toward Brendan as he rounded a corner down the hall. "So how are things going with Brendan? Anything making sense? You feel any better?"

I was amused at Sammy's ability to fire off several questions at once. I wonder what she did before she had the restaurant. *Talk show host? Did she go to college? Is she from here? Is she married? Divorced? Does she have any kids?*

"You know, Sammy, I *am* feeling a little better. I can't say I'm better. I still feel down and a bit anxious... and I'm not really sure how this is going to end." I glanced from her to the floor, taking a deep breath. "But overall, I like being here and listening to Brendan. I met Benny yesterday and that was pretty cool. He seems like someone who has it together."

"Oh, yeah. Benny's a great guy, but he'll tell you that it wasn't always like it is now. You should chat with him some more."

I nodded. "Yeah, he alluded to that. So what about you, Sammy? What's your story?"

She rolled her eyes. "Oh, my story's nothing spectacular. I'll tell you about it later. Right now we've got some painting to do." She placed her arm around my shoulder and led me down the hall.

No sooner had we turned the first corner when we heard a voice behind us. "I hope you came to work today. No goofing off, Samster."

I turned to see Noah rolling toward us quickly, putting on the brakes just in time before the metal foot rests would have collided with my shins.

"Well, hello, Noah." Sammy bent down, and kissed his cheek. "And how are you? Any treatments today? Or can you help us paint?"

"Unfortunately, I do have a treatment and I'll be a little tired after that. I say unfortunately because, as you know, I'm an excellent painter." He glanced at me from head to toe and continued as he turned to Sammy with a sly grin. "And from the looks of this guy, Samster, you could use some help."

Sammy was laughing out loud as he held up his hand for a high five.

"Well, excuse me. I didn't pack my painting clothes when I left Pennsylvania." Their laughter continued.

Noah looked to Sammy. "You guys are painting the old storage room today, right?"

"Yep. You wanna stop by later and give us your approval?"

"Sounds good." He looked at me. "I gotta go, now. On my way to see Vanessa before my treatment."

"Vanessa? Why are you going to see Vanessa? Brendan said I'd be talking with her today."

"You will. Follow me." He grabbed the wheels of his chair and gave it a quick spin.

I looked at Sammy, who flashed a smile and joined the parade as we both followed the wheelchair rolling swiftly down the hallway. Noah rolled his chair in a sweeping arch through an open door. As we approached I noticed that the room was lit only by candles, and there was music playing—soft music, without lyrics.

I turned to look at Sammy, who now had her index finger over her lips. Moving to the doorway, my eyes began to adjust to the dim glow from the many candles scattered throughout the room. There were all shapes, sizes and colors. Some were long and narrow, some short and wide with several wicks.

The room was square with no windows. Spread all around the room were five children: two in wheelchairs and three in brown leather chairs. Noah joined them, closing his eyes. On a stool in the center of the room sat a woman. Her bare feet peeked out from white, baggy pants and she wore a brown sleeveless top. Countless bracelets covered her wrists. Her shoulder-length black and grey hair was pulled back into a ponytail, bound by a brown leather strap. Her eyes were closed and the lines around her eyes and mouth flickered in the soft light.

I turned to Sammy again. "What's this?"

She stared past me through the open doorway. "They're just taking some time out of their day to visit with Vanessa. Some of them are getting better, some are really sick. The children come several times a week just to slow down. It's a time they all look forward to. You should chat with a few of them."

"They just come here to do nothing."

Sammy nodded. "Exactly." Her eyes were fixed on the small occupants of the room.

We stood for the better part of five minutes just watching. Vanessa moved around the room slowly, silently. She stopped at each child. To some she bent down and whispered in their ear. To others, she rubbed her hands together for a few seconds and then held them on the back of a neck. To one small girl with beautiful light brown curly hair, she simply knelt down and placed her cheek on the child's. There they stayed. Quiet. Still. Cheek to cheek.

I watched, surprised that the children didn't flinch or open their eyes.

Sammy poked me in the side lightly and motioned me to follow. We backed away from the doorway slowly, still watching the kids in the room—like parents backing away from the crib of a sleeping infant that had finally fallen back to sleep. Once down the hall Sammy turned. "We'd better get started on this painting."

We gathered our supplies, taped off the windows and molding and discussed our roles. Sammy would use the trim brush to "cut in" around the windows, electric outlets, light switches, molding, the corners, and the spot where the ceiling—already a soft, burnt orange color—met the walls. I would roll the walls. The paint was a brownish color named Down Home. Soft music filled the room constantly as we moved back and forth between periods of conversation and silence.

I was wiping off some paint where I'd rolled past the tape when I heard that now recognizable voice. I looked up from my kneeling position next to the baseboard.

"You're not done yet? Unbelievable. Looks to me like the roller guy's the bottleneck. But the lines look awesome."

Noah rolled past me wearing a slight grin as I grabbed a nearby brush and gestured that I was going to flick paint on him. Entering the room behind him was Vanessa. She walked slowly, her face serene. Something seemed to change when she entered the room. Maybe this is what people mean when they say you know when someone has entered the room. Maybe this is what's meant when folks talk about charisma.

Noah was talking with Sammy, who'd handed him a roller. She stood behind him, both hands on his chair, speaking encouragement as he rolled some paint on the wall.

Vanessa approached me and I began to stand.

"No, no, don't get up, Jake, I'm Vanessa. Brendan asked that we chat a bit today." She lowered herself in one fluid motion to sit cross legged on the floor next to me. "So how are you?"

"Well, other than the fact that Noah thinks I am a lousy painter, I'm pretty good."

She smiled. "Ah, yes, my dear friend Noah." She glanced at him and then back to me. "How about everything else?"

"Oh that. I guess you spoke with Brendan." I was getting used to having complete strangers knowing more about me than I'd normally be comfortable with. But I hadn't come here to be comfortable.

"Absolutely," said Vanessa. "Brendan told me you've had a tough time the past several months. I think it's really interesting that you connected with Paul in North Carolina, and then found your way out here to spend time with Brendan."

"Well, I must say I'm starting to feel a little better. I don't quite have the vision thing down that Brendan talked about, you know, to get real clear on where I'm headed so it might be easier to see the path. Then there's the other part where I need to take some action to get on the path."

Vanessa nodded. "The action is the path."

"Yeah, I guess it is." *Hmm, never thought about it that way.* "I feel like I've been saying this a lot lately, but I'm trying to figure this all out. I'm hoping that Brendan's Jackrabbit thing might serve me well—both in getting out of the rut I'm in now and maybe even after that."

"I think you'll find that Brendan's 'Jackrabbit thing' has helped a lot of people, myself included."

"You too?" I said incredulously.

She laughed. "Yes... me, Sammy, Benny... and others around here you'll meet sooner or later. I'm betting that most of the people you've met so far are very sympathetic to what you're going through. It's because we've all been through something similar. Maybe not the exact struggles, but moments of profound confusion."

I was still stunned. "You? Profound confusion?"

She laughed again. "Yes, even me."

"And Brendan helped you?"

"Maybe what's true is that we've helped each other. I've known Brendan for a long time and he's a very good thinker. And remember that the way we think—good or not so good—is our foundation for action. But you're getting me off track. I promised Brendan that I'd talk with you for a little while about energy." She touched my arm, and looked deeply into my eyes.

"What do you mean by energy?"

"Good question. How about you answer first, then I'll go?"

I shifted my position on the floor. "I guess energy—to me— is sort of how we feel. You know how we feel if we're eating right and getting some good rest. And I guess it's also kind of connected to our outlook on things, you know, half-full or half-empty. To me it's important because we need physical energy in our day to day lives."

Vanessa pulled her legs in closer to her body. "Sure, great answer. But I'd like to offer something additional for you to consider. Jake, there's an energy that we all have the opportunity to access, and its usually very individual for people. It's available when we slow down and disengage from our physical world and the distractions that this world produces. Some people call it connecting with their soul, while others believe it's their ability to get in touch with the Holy Spirit, that extension of God that's a source of strength to many of us. Nonetheless, many people access this energy daily. It's routine for them, and they cannot be without it." She said "cannot" very slowly, and paused before she finished. "Life flows better when we're connected to it."

It was easy to listen to Vanessa. Her words and tones were warm and inviting. "Okay, I think I kind of know what you're talking about. I go to church and feel pretty good there sometimes. Well, I used to go, but I'm not into it too much these days."

"Yes, there's definitely some great energy available in churches, but not only there. This energy can be accessed all over."

"Is it hard to do? Does it take a long time?"

"No, not really, there are many possibilities. Sometimes we get on the floor or a mat and get very still. Some have more of a religious nature, like prayer. Some are of a spiritual nature—not through formal prayer—but just through a conscious effort to get free of thoughts. Others practice this through becoming immersed in the solitude of nature—a walk as the sun rises over some eastern horizon or disappears into a shimmering sea. Sometimes it's just a morning walk through the woods to do the trick."

I jumped in. "This must have been what Paul was doing on our last morning when we stood at the ocean's edge in North Carolina. He asked if we could just enjoy the sunrise without talking."

"Yes, Paul knows this." She paused. "Perhaps even more so, now. Many people over the years have grown to understand the importance of this ritual. Albert Einstein was probably speaking of this when he said, 'I have lived in solitude in the country and noticed how the monotony of a quiet life stimulates the creative mind.' People don't often realize that slowing down can actually help them get to where they are going more easily and quickly. Sometimes"—she winked "—one of the most productive activities around getting something done is actually doing nothing."

I felt myself embracing the comforting feeling of being with this woman. "Does this work for anybody? Or just sick people and geniuses?"

"Oh, it's beneficial for anyone who commits to it. I've directed most of my recent focus to helping people with physical illness—mostly children—because, for me, there's something unnatural about a child being sick. In my mind, children should be full of energy, wonder, and excitement. They should be able to run and jump and laugh and learn. It really hits me in a deep place in my soul when a sickness impedes this in these beautiful young people." Vanessa glanced at Sammy, then Noah, then back to me.

"Actually, Jake, corporate America is beginning to get a bit more interested in the physical, mental, and spiritual well-being of their people. Can you believe companies are now allowing the word spiritual to be used? It used to be forbidden! So many companies today are screaming—literally in some cases—for innovation and energy from their people, yet these folks receive hundreds of distracting and worthless emails per day—then they attend far too many meetings in an eight hour workday. How does that happen? Even if they work a ten-hour day, five to eight hours of meetings? How are they supposed to get their work done? I believe one of the greatest opportunities for these folks is to create pockets of time throughout the day to just be still. The people that I work with that have begun to develop these rituals, and they all say they re-engage with their work with greater focus and relaxation."

I thought about a brief stint in corporate America at a credit card bank I worked at for a few years before the accident, and some of the folks there that just ran, ran, ran all day. Yeah, some of those people would definitely benefit from chilling out for a bit. "So this seems to work?"

"Let me say this, Jake. I've written many articles on executive coaching and performance, and on holistic living and healing. I've even written a few books. My coaching fee with companies is $10,000 per day, and I'm turning down requests every week. I'm telling you this so you know where I am right now. This isn't about ego. I gave that up a long time ago, thankfully. Here's the point. I won't work with anyone—no matter how much money they offer me—who will not begin to explore, or continue exploring, the power of having rituals that enable them to get to a quiet place."

"You feel that strongly about this?"

"Absolutely. I like to think that I just know this is right, and valuable."

"So is journaling the same kind of thing?" I asked. "I know a guy, pretty cool guy actually. I used to think he was a bit of a nut, not really grounded in reality. But over the years he's created a pretty nice and successful life for himself. He's a big fan of journaling. He used to tell me it was just good for him to write out what he was thinking about, said it was great to go back and read what he wrote several months or years later."

Vanessa straightened her legs, leaning forward to grab her toes. She stayed like this for a few seconds, and then sat straight. "Great insight. Journaling works well for many people, a little for some, and not at all for others. Remember, Jake that the principles of Jackrabbit are simple, and this simplicity offers many ways by which to practice them. Many executives I work with who begin to practice stillness just close their doors and put their head back two or three times a day. Their sole focus during this time is to be aware of their breathing. Period. Others go outside and find a bench or wall on which to rest a bit. Personally, I've found that converting my thoughts to words on paper is time well spent. But it's the stillness that's most important. Not the writing. Just *being* with yourself can provide joy, focus, creativity, gratitude, humor, healing, and vision!"

Though open to the idea, I was still skeptical. "That sounds like a lot of positives to pile on to something as simple as putting my head back a few times a day..."

She nodded at me. "Yes, it is. And nothing I can say will convince you. It's like what Brendan always says—*telling* isn't the best way of learning. You have to experience these things for yourself."

Just then two small hands came from behind Vanessa and wrapped around her neck. Vanessa turned. "Well, if it isn't my dear little friend Sophie. I've been waiting all day to see your smiling face. Sophie, this is my new friend, Jake."

I found myself face to face with a young girl, who was, indeed, smiling. I smiled back and took her outstretched hand.

Vanessa held onto Sophie's hand as she turned to me. "Jake, I need to take Sophie to spend some time alone. Perhaps we can talk again while you're out here. Or if you think you understand the importance of what I've talked to you about, and what Brendan has so simply captured in his Jackrabbit philosophy, then my only wish is that you begin to implement this into your life..." she paused, her warm eyes going from Sophia to me. "In whatever way makes sense to you. Just experiment with it—then reflect on how the experiment works. I think it will. I've shared with you a little about stillness. You got information here. You'll get wisdom out there." Vanessa gestured outside. "Make sense?"

I paused. "Yes. I think I may get a bit wiser when I begin to apply some of what I'm learning."

Vanessa stood as Sophie clung to her waist. I got to my feet, welcoming Vanessa's outstretched arms and the three of us stood for a long moment in a hug. I felt a little uncomfortable, but didn't want to be the first one to break the contact.

"Yes, Vanessa. I do believe it makes sense. Thank you so much."

She smiled and kissed me on the cheek. "Be well, Jake. This will all be okay." She turned and grabbed Sophie's hand as the two of them moved down the hall.

I wasn't sure it would all be okay. I thought back to the first day I'd arrived in Moab, when I was sitting in my truck at Sammy's place. I remembered the guy who walked out the back door, put the trash in the dumpster, closed his eyes and turned his face to the sun. *Well, he was just taking a break. This must work for everyone, no matter what their position in life. And that guy looked really happy. I wonder if this is what I was doing when I stopped by the river and laid down on the rock. I guess I was slowing down, and it certainly did seem to recharge my battery.* I recalled another quote from Einstein, "I want to know God's thoughts, the rest are details."

I walked toward Sammy. "Looked like some good time over there on the floor with Vanessa. Ready to get back to work?"

"Sure, let's get back to it. Vanessa sure is cool, and she speaks so calmly for someone with such strong conviction."

Sammy leaned down to grab a paintbrush. "Yes, she's one of the special ones, for sure."

We worked until about 4 o'clock and actually finished the room—in spite of our many visitors.

As we climbed into her Jeep at the end of the day I thought about how much I loved these vehicles, especially the soft-top. Nothing quite like a ride in a Jeep with the top down. I glanced over at Sammy—her hair blowing a little from the soft breeze—as we pulled out of the Tuscany lot.

14

Sammy's Story

"We dare not disregard the lessons of experience."
–Abraham Lincoln

I looked over at Sammy, her face speckled with paint. As we rolled down the highway I spoke loudly over the rushing wind. "So what about you?"

"I'm sorry?"

"So how'd you wind up here? My first day here you were talking about the wonderful influence Brendan has been to so many people. And you said, 'Myself included.'"

"Oh, yeah, that." She grinned a little ruefully. "Guess I can't avoid giving an answer this time, can I?"

"Nope. *The time has come to talk of many things…*" I quoted.

She turned off the road into the desert, rolled to a stop, and turned off the engine. We sat for a moment, watching the sun begin to drop behind the distant hills. "Well, Jake, you asked, so here's my story."

I unclicked my seatbelt and turned toward her. Sammy did the same, took a deep breath in through her nose and let it escape with a whooshing sound that rushed through her parted lips.

"Well, it was a number of years ago. I was working on Wall Street at a powerhouse firm. I'd been with them for four years and was the youngest female in the history of the firm to be promoted to Managing Director. From what I heard, many of the people there thought it was because I'd slept with the right people." She stared into the distance and laughed, and then grew silent.

I summoned the nerve to ask the question. "Well, did you?"

She laughed again, loudly. "Jake, let me set one thing straight. I like money, always did, always will—just for different reasons now. Money in and of itself is not a bad thing. It's the process by which we go about making it—and what we do with it—where many people get off track. This is where I've seen a lot of good people do bad things. If you could've seen some of the guys I supposedly slept with…" Sammy did the quote thing with her fingers when she said slept. "They were all very jaded. Well, there's a limit to what I'll do for the almighty dollar. No, Jake, I did not sleep my way to Managing Director.

"Anyhow, the time was crazy—in a good way. It was a great time to be on Wall Street. The year ended and it was my first one where I made over two million dollars."

I winced. "Two million? Whoa."

"Yep. Crazy, huh? The question with many stocks was not if you were going to make money, but *how much*. And the big question was when to get out? The swings were nutty, really unpredictable. Anyhow, my coworkers and I went out one night in early spring, a few months after my promotion, and had a great party—limos, dinner, champagne, everything... a real celebration. I'd finished a great year and was on my way to making even more money. I guess I got home around three in the morning and passed out."

Sammy had awoken the next morning with a dry mouth and a head feeling like a spike had been driven through it. She went to get coffee at this small shop around the corner, and it was there she just stared into her soy latte.

"I just had one thought going through my brain—what am I doing?" Sammy said. "Well, just then my phone rings and it's my best friend Alexis. She's a hairstylist in Manhattan and she starts talking away. I interrupt her after about thirty seconds—I hadn't heard a word she said—and asked her 'Lex, what am I doing?' 'What?' she said. I repeated, 'what the hell am I doing with my life?'"

"She asked simply, 'Sammy, what are you talking about?'

"'Lex,' I said, 'I'm sitting here at the coffee shop. I was out late last night celebrating the fact that I'm making a lot of money. I probably spent about five thousand of it last night.'

"Then I paused for a moment, and tears came to my eyes. I remember it like it was yesterday. I said, 'I have everything that I need on the outside, but it's just occurred to me—or just surfaced—that I don't have anything on the inside." Sammy's voice softened and her head shook as she finished. There was silence.

I wasn't sure what to say and managed only a faint "Wow."

"Yeah. Wow. It was kind of like the lyrics from a singer I like, Susan Tedeschi, when she sings, 'I found out, after a while, reading those books was making me lose my smile.' I think that what I was doing was making me lose my smile, my inherent sense of joy...my sense of purpose.

"Well, Lex came down and had some coffee with me and we spent about two hours together. I'll bet there are many life-altering conversations held in coffee shops. Maybe it's the whole beatnik, Jack Kerouac thing. Anyhow, the up-shot was that Lex determined I needed a vacation. I told her I'd already been— the islands, Hawaii, Paris, Amsterdam, I mean many great places... the Keys....man, a great place. All these trips were okay, but they wore off, usually by day two back on Wall Street."

"So what'd you do?"

"Well, I told her I wasn't in the mood to go on vacation. But I thought she may be onto something. I told her I had a better idea. I wanted to get into my Porsche, drop the top, and head to the end of New Jersey, to exit zero of the Garden State Parkway. Lex looked at me like I'd lost my mind. She said, 'Exit what?'

"'Exit zero', I told her. The last exit going south on the Garden State Parkway, right by Cape May. You can drive into Cape May, onto the ferry that crosses over to Delaware, or into the Delaware Bay.' Anyhow, I packed that Thursday night and took off around two o'clock the next day. I booked into a room at a great bed & breakfast, an old Victorian place with purple awnings, a block off the town mall. I went for long walks on the beach, had a few drinks at the local spots. To me, it's really a great thing to get away—alone—where nobody knows you." She pointed her finger at me. "I began to relax, I mean really relax and it was wonderful. Anyhow—and bear with me here, Jake, you're the one who asked how I wound up here in Moab."

I nodded and raised my hands in surrender. "Hey, keep going, I'm intrigued. I used to go to Ocean City when I was growing up and spent some time in Avalon, too, so I know Cape May a bit. I just forgot about the exit zero thing."

"So one night I decide to go to one of my favorite places in Cape May, the Lobster House. It's a huge restaurant right on the water with commercial fishing boats docked all around. There's a rumor that Oprah sometimes docks her yacht there because she owns a house a few towns over. Not sure if that's true, but it's a good story! Out back there's a large blue and white sailboat that's permanently docked, called The Schooner. It doesn't move. It's just an extension of the restaurant, with a great bar up on the bow and tables sprinkled about the deck. It must be over 80 feet long. So I go to the place—which is always packed—and get a rare parking space right out front, and head to the Schooner."

Sammy leaned back in the car seat, closing her eyes as her mind drifted back to the past. "I can remember it as clearly as if I were still sitting there," she said. "As I walked up to the deck, I passed a photo on the wall of an old boat named Skilligolee tied up to a dock, surrounded by tanned and smiling men. A handwritten note underneath said that 'skilligolee' meant 'white marlin' in a Native American language. Up on the deck, a huge seagull sat on the old, weathered cedar roof, right above the faded letters of their sign, THE RAW BAR. I think it was waiting for a stray french fry or oyster cracker. I could see half a dozen boats tied up at the docks— the *Mary Anne, Mary Hazel, Ruby's Pride & Joy, Susan L* and *Negotiator*. I don't know if I had a premonition that the day was going to be special in my life, but for some reason I pulled out a small notebook while I sat at the bar and wrote everything down.

"I'm not there five minutes when an older woman sits down next to me. She said hello, asked if it was OK if she sat by me because she hated sitting alone in bars. I said it was fine and we began to chat. Her name was Ginny. On my second glass of wine I begin to tell her about that feeling of burnout I was experiencing. Turns out she was from Ohio and had been coming to Cape May with her husband and family for over thirty years. After a lull in our conversation she turns to me and asks, 'So, my dear Samantha, what are you going to do?'

"I respond with the all too familiar line many of us give when facing challenges, 'I don't know.' Ginny let out a sigh and asked another question, 'What if you did know?' I said, 'What if I did know what I was going to do next? … Well, I guess next for me would include talking to someone who would understand and maybe help me figure things out. Nobody around me seems to get it.'"

"Ah… so you did know where I was coming from that first day I was here," I said.

Sammy nodded slightly. "You're not the only one to get lost, Jake. Anyway, Ginny turned to me and looked directly into my eyes and said, 'If you're serious about that, I know someone who you can speak with.' She told me that the man was a friend of her husband's."

"Wait a minute." I interrupted. "Isn't … I mean, wasn't Ginny the name of Paul's wife?"

"Bingo! The one and only, and what a wonderful woman. Can you believe that I came to know Brendan because I met Paul's wife, Ginny, on a boat behind a restaurant in Cape May, New Jersey?"

I didn't hesitate. "Sure I can, because I met Paul when he popped out of a wave in Kill Devil Hills, North Carolina, on the Outer Banks. Man, it's like these people are everywhere, on the lookout for screwed up people like us."

She smacked my shoulder and laughed. "Well, Ginny and I had a wonderful dinner, during which I learned a little about Brendan. But I still wasn't sure what he really did or was all about. Afterward, I gave her my email address."

I recalled my frustration with Paul and his vague description of Brendan and his work. "Sounds familiar," I said.

"I stayed in Cape May for another day and then made the trek back north. Later that week, Ginny sent me an email with Brendan's address—no phone number or email, just an old-fashioned street address. And she mentioned something about Jackrabbit, which of course meant nothing to me since she never talked about it at dinner.

"To this day I don't know why I didn't delete that email from Ginny with Brendan's address on it, like I did with so many other 'follow-up' emails. I mean who just sends a person's address as their contact information? No phone? Cell phone? Email? Website? But for some reason I dragged it over to a folder I created called Jackrabbit, just one email, in one folder, all alone."

"You didn't act on it then?"

"Nope, I forgot about it for probably six months until one day it happened." Sammy paused, looked away from me to the ground, and then began again.

"I was on the trading floor—the market was making a big run—and I was going full tilt, on my third cup of coffee for the morning. I hadn't eaten a thing. I was sitting in a chair watching the board. It was crazy, people running around, noise everywhere. And suddenly, I didn't see the chaos anymore, or hear the voices calling out to buy or sell. I just sat there in silence, staring at the board. I don't know how long I sat there. I guess it lasted a few minutes or so. Just silence. Finally, I got up and walked outside, got in my car, and drove. I ended up in New Hampshire this time. God, the memory is still so clear."

"Seems you have a notion to take a drive when things get crazy. I'm familiar with the running away tactic."

Sammy smiled slightly. "Yeah, I thought you might be. I still love to take drives, but more now to see, or discover something—rather than trying to get away from something. The next day I drove back to New York and told my boss I was leaving."

"What'd he say?"

"He's a good guy, a very committed husband and father. We still stay in touch. But he did what many well-intentioned people do. He suggested a shallow solution to a deep situation. In short, he convinced me to stay. He's a brilliant salesman.

"What do you mean a 'shallow solution'?"

"He said I could take the rest of the week off then come back on Monday. Since I didn't really have any better idea, I agreed with that plan. But after our talk I returned to my computer and began to plow through emails and for some reason my focus shifted to the Jackrabbit folder on the bottom left of the screen, it was toward the bottom, right below investment strategy. As I sat staring at the folder, I remembered a great piece of wisdom a priest friend of mine had given me many years before. He told me not to worry so much about finding the answers to life's questions, because when you think you've got them, the questions change."

"Hmm, I like that."

"Yeah, me too. Anyhow, I realized that while I was looking for answers in the chaotic energy of Wall Street a new question had arisen— WHY? Why am I here? Why am I doing what I'm doing? Why do I feel a real lack a lack of happiness and fulfillment? Just WHY?

"So I pulled out one of my note cards, the ones with my initials—SJW—on top. Jake, you have to understand, these note cards are very special to me and I choose who I send them to very carefully." She reached into her back pocket and pulled out a crumpled and beat up envelope. She pulled a note from inside and read to me:

> *"Dear Brendan –*
> *You don't know me. I received your name and address from Ginny last summer in Cape May, New Jersey. My name is Samantha and I work on Wall Street in NYC. I'm twenty-nine years old and I've just realized that up to this point my life has been void of any deep personal reflection, actually very little reflection at all. Well, now I think I need to go deep, if you know what I mean. Ginny said you have a gift for helping people. Any chance I might visit you in Utah to meet and talk?*
> *Sincerely,*
> *Samantha Windermere*

Sammy had included her email address and sent the letter. A week had passed, during which she fell right back into her old routines—work, sleep, work, and sleep.

"I'd pretty much forgotten about Brendan when the email from him arrived. An excitement from deep within me surfaced, like when I was in high school and I knew this guy I liked was going to ask me to the prom. It was something I hadn't felt in a long time. I remember hesitating before I clicked the mouse to open it. I guess I slipped into some negative self-talk about him not having time for me, or just giving a standard one-sentence reply, a pleasant brush-off."

Sammy paused for drama, smirking at me and my noticeable anticipation. "So what did it say?" I was forced by curiosity to ask.

"I remember it by heart. It said...

Sammy – I received your note. Ginny told me about you and the dinner you two had in Cape May. Our conversation brought back wonderful memories of some time I spent there one summer. I love the Schooner out back of the Lobster House; wonderful when the wind dies and the slick calm of the water is broken by a slow-moving, fishing boat.

Anyhow, I will be in Utah this month. How's next Monday? I'll meet you at noon at a restaurant in Moab called The Grille. Just ask anybody in town, they'll be able to tell you where it is.

Lunch is on me. We can talk then. I'll wait to hear from you.

Be well.

Brendan

"Wow, I thought. And the email had a great logo of a Jackrabbit in the signature area. Something about the email made me go to my calendar, clear it for the next Monday and Tuesday, and then call my travel agent. Within twenty minutes, I'd booked my trip to Moab and responded to Brendan's email. And a few days later I found myself here."

"So you came out and met with Brendan. And he started teaching you about Jackrabbit, just like he's doing with me, right? "

"Yes, like you I had some time with him. I'm not going to tell you what we talked about, but I will admit that I changed my flight home several times and wound up staying here for eleven days on my first visit. I had a great time and really got to a place deep inside my soul. A place I don't think I'd ever come close to before. Turns out I had the answers all along. We often do. I just wasn't asking myself the proper questions, or giving myself the space to hear them."

"I still don't quite get it. What do you mean going deep inside your soul?"

"You'll have to talk to Brendan about that," she answered, a cryptic smile on her lips.

"And just like that you were fixed?"

Sammy laughed. "Not quite. I just gave you the short version of the story. I returned to New York for about six months, sold my condo, and then went to the Florida Keys for another six. Then I came out here. I lived at the hotel in town awhile and then decided to buy the restaurant where Brendan and I met. I moved into the apartment upstairs there."

"You bought The Grille? The place you first met Brendan?"

"Yep. The sweet old couple that had owned it for years wanted to sell and get closer to their grandkids in Kansas City. It worked out for both of us."

"And you've stayed here ever since? Never gone back?"

"One question at a time, Jake. Yes, I've stayed here ever since. I've traveled to other places, of course, but Moab has become my home."

"And are you ever going back?"

"Think about what you're asking, Jake. You're implying that somehow living here in Moab is a retreat from the real world, but in fact I've found that for me being here is more real than Wall Street ever was. But..." she paused.

"But..." I prompted.

"But, I have been thinking lately that maybe it's time to try something new. You've talked to Brendan about vision, right?" I nodded, and she continued. "Well my vision a few years ago was to come here and be still with myself and with the world. And it's worked out very well. I get to meet a lot of great people all the time, and help out with the center. But I think maybe I need a new vision now. It's been easy to be still here in Moab. I'm wondering if I can keep the stillness even if I go to a busier place.

"And I will say that I have no regrets about coming or even for the reasons I needed to come. Regret is nothing more than a negative feeling about the past. The only thing we can do with the past is learn from it and, of course, retrieve some great memories. I'm actually continually grateful for having paid attention—for being aware—of the fact that something was missing in my life. I guess I'm thankful for that hangover in the coffee shop. That's why I carry the note I sent Brendan, just to keep me aware. He gave it back to me the day I bought The Grille."

15

Confession

"Misfortunes come to all men."

–Chinese proverb

I felt Sammy's stare as I studied the desert shadows, noticing they were growing longer. "Now it's your turn," she said after awhile.

"Sorry?"

"I just told you my story. Now I want to hear yours. What happened that brought you here?"

I shrugged, got out of the Jeep, made my way to the front, and took a seat on the bumper. I'd not told anyone other than my family and very close friends about the accident and Brian's death. And telling them wasn't easy. I got drunk after every telling. I didn't even tell Paul the whole story. I looked to the distance, my mind racing.

Sammy joined me on the bumper. "You know, you don't have to tell me if you don't want to. We can just stay here a little longer, enjoying the end of day here in the desert, and then head back."

I took a deep breath, for sure one of the deepest of my life, and began.

"There was an accident. I was electrocuted. Well,"—I laughed sarcastically—"maybe not electrocuted. One doctor in the hospital clarified for me that I was electrically burned, not electrocuted. Electrocution—he told me—results in death. He was an arrogant young guy. I mean there I was lying in the hospital with tubes and lines in just about every opening of my body, and this dude was giving me a vocabulary lesson. At that point, I didn't give a crap about the difference. All I knew was one minute I was trying to finish up work so I could meet some buddies to play nine holes of golf. Then the next minute I'm in the ICU pretty messed up, and not just physically."

Sammy's voice was just a whisper. "What happened?"

"Well, I was working for some friends of mine, Brian and Steve. They were brothers who had a successful roofing business they'd taken over from their dad, great old guy, quite a character. I'd been trying to start my own business selling an item I'd invented called the Beach Belt. It was a carrying strap for beach chairs and accessories. Like I said, we used to go to the shore as a kid."

"I can tell you're from the East," Sammy said. "We're the only ones who call it the shore. Drives my friends from LA crazy. They cannot get over it. 'It's the beach,' they say, 'not the shore.'"

"Yes, it definitely seems to be a Philly/Jersey thing.

"Anyhow, I was trying to get this business going, selling beach chairs with college logos printed on them. But business wasn't exactly booming. So to make money I was tending bar and working a few days a week for Brian and Steve. It was a good job. Outdoors, nice and physical, good pay, and Brian and Steve were great guys. Both were married, but only Brian had kids at the time, he had three. His youngest daughter was just a few months old."

I sat there thinking of all the things Brian's kids could no longer be doing with their dad. "I've thought about the day of the accident a lot, but I'm still not quite sure how it happened. We were setting up this thing called a laddervator. It looks like a regular aluminum ladder except it's about twenty-eight-feet long and has a motor and hoist on it that sends supplies up to the roof so you don't have to carry them up."

I explained to her that the laddervator comes in one section and can't be collapsed like a regular ladder. When we put it up each day, we'd lean the top of it against the roofline. Then to take it down, we had to do a reverse tilt, with one person stabilizing the feet of the ladder as the other grabbed as high up as he could and then walked backwards, shifting his grip as he walked, until he could grab the end that had been the top. And then we'd load it back onto the truck.

"Anyway, I'd been the one stabilizing the base of the ladder. But at the end of the day, Brian started taking off his tool belt on the way to the truck and he yelled over to me that he'd be back to help take down the laddervator in a minute. It was a hot day and I was real thirsty, so I went to get a drink of water from my jug. As I turned and headed back to the laddervator I saw that Brian had taken my spot, propping his feet against the base of the ladder. So I went to the other side of the ladder, and grabbed on. He pushed and I pulled, and I started walking backwards, enough so that the top of the ladder pulled back from the top of the roof until it was sticking straight up in the air. We were less than two feet from each other. 'Good?' Brian asked. Good. I said.

"I then began to walk backwards holding the ladder above my head as its sides slid through my hands. He said we were looking good.

"And that's when it happened. All I remember is being hit by a surge of something—I wasn't sure what—that instantly tore through my entire body. My first thought was that I'd been shot, or that there had been a nuclear accident. The investigators afterward said we'd hit some power lines. We'd noticed them earlier in the day but thought we had plenty of clearance. But when the ladder hit those wires, we got hit with between 10,000 and 13,000 volts."

I paused, took a deep breath and let it slowly out and leaned my head back until it rested on the hood. My eyes filled, my face tightened.

Sammy placed her hand on my shoulder. "Hey Jake, it's okay. You don't need to tell me anymore. We can talk about it later if you want."

I nodded, wiping my eyes with the back of my hand. "Thanks, but I'll be alright. After I had this thought of being shot or there having been a nuclear accident, things got a bit strange, but in a good way, sort of. I was never nervous or filled with anxiety or fear. The first thing I did was yell to Steve, 'Steve, get Brian. Steve, get Brian.'" My voice was a hoarse whisper.

"Then I—or some part of me—I think it was my soul, began to rise above my body. I was looking down at...at... at me! But I wasn't really me anymore. Steve told me afterward that when he got to me I was as dead as he ever imagined a dead person being. He said when he got to me I wasn't breathing and he couldn't find a heartbeat. My eyes were rolled back in my head, and I was foaming at the mouth. He told me he kept thinking, *We killed Jake.*" I paused, taking a few deep breaths.

"Jake, that sounds just awful. I don't know what to say. I feel like I'm trying to think of something to say but I can't. I'm just stuck here looking at the sun reflecting in your eyes. I just don't know what to say. This is crazy."

I turned. "Sammy, it's okay. I'm just glad you're here."

"Yeah, me too. I mean not that I'm here, but that you are. I mean I'm glad to be here too. Sorry, I'm all mixed up."

I put my hand on hers. "Me, too, Sammy. But while Steve was crouching over me, I didn't really see him. You see, I'd been rising up… and was no longer in my body. I think…no…I know and believe that I was with God."

Sammy closed her eyes, biting her bottom lip. "No shit."

My smile was sad. "You can say that again."

"Sorry, I don't mean to curse. I hardly do it anymore, used to curse like a sailor when I was in New York. I just mean, I've never met someone who has…"

"Died." I filled in the blank.

"Yeah, I guess. I mean I've known people who have died, but then again they were dead. I've just never met someone who died, and then came back."

"Yeah, me neither."

"Except yourself."

"I guess."

We sat together on the bumper, her face closer to mine than when she'd first sat down. "So what's God like?"

"Good question. He—or she—I'm not sure, isn't a gray-haired, bearded old man, at least not to me. That's how I thought about God when I was young. I didn't see a light, or my great aunt and her purple hair, or anybody else for that matter. I was just ..." I searched for a word, the right word. "I was just in a state of absolute peace. I guess that's the best word I can come up with, although peace doesn't do it justice. I—that spiritual essence that continues when our body stops—was connected to something, or someone... beautiful."

"Sammy," I said, looking directly at her, "it was the greatest feeling and emotion I ever experienced. I didn't want it to end. Think about the time in your life when you felt the greatest emotion, or power, or impact of Love, then multiply that by a thousand. Then you're getting close to the experience I had."

She sat there on the bumper, just shaking her head. "Did you talk with God?"

"Not really talked, no words were exchanged. I mean I didn't see anyone. I was just with a beautiful source of energy, of Love. It was more like we communicated than spoke. You know how sometimes you can read someone's thoughts, and they yours?" She nodded. "Well that's where we were, and at a very, very sophisticated level. It moved quickly. I can't say I was in a physical space because I wasn't physical. I was 'floating,' but not my body, because it was lying on the ground lifeless. 'Me' was no longer 6'1" and 170 pounds. 'Me' was some form of energy, a conscious energy. I could remember my life on Earth, but I was definitely no longer in it. We reviewed my life—the good that I did, as well as the not so good. I didn't want to come back to this world."

I paused at this statement, and then repeated it, "I did not want to come back to this world. And I let God know this."

"So why did you? Come back, I mean?"

"I'm not sure." I gave a small laugh as I heard myself say the words that Sammy had used not long ago. "That's probably why I'm here. The funny thing about all of this, if any of it can be called funny, is that everything changed when I asked, or communicated to God, 'What about Lauren and what about my mom?' And boom! Suddenly I was back in my body."

"Who's Lauren?"

"She was... is, maybe... my girlfriend. We'd been dating on and off for about six years. I wasn't ... still aren't... sure what's going on between us. But I thought about her in that moment. Her and my mom."

"I think most people would think about their mothers at a time like that."

"That may be, but my mom and I have always had a strong bond. I know my dad loves me, too, but it's no secret in the family that I'm my mom's favorite. My brothers are always busting my butt about it, yelling out to me 'My Jake' in her high tones."

I took another deep breath then continued. "I've read a few books and articles about people who've had experiences similar to mine, and there's a strong theme that suggests we come back when we express concern for others. That's what happened with me. The instance I no longer solely thought about myself, but wondered what would happen to the people I loved, I was back in my body. To me, as I've reflected on this the past few months — even drunk — it's all about Love. The greatest thing we can do is Love, and serve others. I never asked to come back because I hadn't made my millions, or because I'd never bought the sports car I wanted. I just simply expressed my Love for another — in my case two people.

"Well, anyhow, it was at this point that I came back into my body. You ever see a movie where this happens?" Sammy nodded. "Well, old Hollywood got it right in this case. I remember hearing Steve yelling 'Brian... Brian... Brian' and slapping Brian's face. It was really weird. My whole body felt as though

I was lying on my side in the fetal position, but actually I was lying flat on my back because I found myself staring straight up at the laddervator above me. You see, it only nicked the high-voltage line by a quarter inch or so and it kept falling. It got caught up on a phone line about ten feet off the ground.

"You know how when your arm falls asleep when you're sleeping and your brain is telling it to move, and nothing happens? That's what happened to me, to my entire body. After a few minutes my body finally began again to do what my brain asked it to, and I was able to get to my hands and knees and crawl to Steve and Brian. I came up next to Steve and he turned to me with wide eyes and said. 'Oh man, you're alive.' Yeah, something like that, I replied.

"Sammy, when I tell you that I will never forget the look, or actually the lack of the look in Brian's eyes, I really mean it. They were wonderfully bright blue and alive normally, and now they were just... just...just there. He was dead. I didn't know how, but I knew why. He was in my place."

My eyes filled and Sammy reached out as I collapsed into her arms, shaking and sobbing violently. I finally settled, pulled away, and continued.

"We worked on Brian for a couple of minutes. Steve was doing the compressions on Brian's chest, I was doing the mouth-to-mouth. We did this for a few minutes until the paramedics arrived, but it wasn't good."

Sammy watched as I got up off the bumper, turned, and walked a few steps away. I spoke in a whisper to the desert and the fading sun. "I will never forget the feeling of his lifeless mouth, and his mustache. I knew he was dead, but I kept trying and trying to make him breathe again ... I kept blowing into his mouth over and over and over again. I couldn't stop. I didn't want to give up. I tried with everything I had to get him to breathe again."

I turned back to Sammy after a minute. "I learned later than Brian got a bigger jolt than I did because he was standing in my place, his feet propped against the ladder. Just that point of contact. The laddervator was just resting on my palms. I wasn't really holding on so the electricity flowed through me, frying my insides a little bit and exited out the sides of my feet. So you see I was right all along. Brian was dead because I'd gone to get a drink of water, a stupid drink of water, and he'd taken my place. His kids no longer have a dad and Steve no longer has a brother. And it's because of me."

I expected Sammy to say the kind of things people usually say when I talk like this. "It wasn't your fault" … "It's just survivors guilt…" But she remained silent, which struck me as a gracious move. She wasn't trying to make me change my mind.

A minute or two later, I continued. "After the paramedics started working on Brian, I crawled over to a fence and just sat there, staring at two small black holes in my boots. I took them off and saw larger holes outlined in black in my socks. Then I took them off and stared into holes in my feet, wondering why there wasn't any blood. Steve came over and I asked him if he'd heard me yelling at him to get Brian, get Brian. Steve just looked at me blankly and said, 'You didn't say anything.'"

I turned away again, shaking my head, sniffles came from Sammy. She hugged me and didn't let go.

16

Change of Plans

"If there is no wind, row."

—Latin proverb

"Can we go now?" I asked. "I'm feeling talked out."

"Sure." We climbed into the Jeep and Sammy turned to me before turning the key, placing her hand on my shoulder. "You're in a good place here, Jake. That was an awful thing that happened to you and Steve and Brian. But if you want to, you will get better."

I tried to smile. "You know, I think I'm starting to believe that, I mean really believe. You know how Brendan talks about one discipline of Jackrabbit being to develop vision?"

"Yep, it's at the center of the philosophy."

"Well, that's the main reason I'm here. The night before I met Paul, I was in a bar. I left after a few beers—well, quite a few beers actually, and a shot or two of tequila thrown in just to be sure I got a good buzz… plus I think I smoked some weed in a parking lot with a guy I happened to be talking to. When I left the bar and stumbled towards my motel, I saw a phone booth sitting under a street light. I'm certain that it wasn't there when I had pulled in a few days earlier. I mean there aren't many phone booths around anymore. Anyhow, I made my way to the phone booth and called my Mom—she wanted to know when I was coming home. That was all she said, that she loved me and wanted to know when I was coming home. I'm sure she could hear in my voice that I was high, but all she did was express her love for me.

"And on the way back to my room I began to think—even though I was pretty ripped—What would it be like if I did go back home? What if I could get better?"

Sammy nodded as she pulled some hair behind her ear. "Yes, that is developing vision, and it's been my experience that when people turn to the future, to possibilities, to what can be, then life begins to get better. It's never easy, but it is good. We all get to a messed up place in life from time to time, we just really need to get good at figuring out what it would look and be like when it's no longer messed up. That's vision. Seems like that's what you started to do that night walking back to your room."

I shook my head. "Yeah, I guess. Here we are, the philosophers of Moab. Are we off to your place to meet Brendan now?"

"Nope. Change of plans." She slapped me on the leg. "You'll see. No more questions. You up for some music or do you want some quiet?"

I nodded. "Sure, music sounds like a good idea." She slid a CD into her radio, hit a few buttons, and pulled her hair into a ponytail. The unmistakable, raspy voice of a New Jersey rocker began to sing about Cadillacs as I looked out the window and the cool desert air hit my face.

During the ride I focused on my breathing, trying to calm myself after recounting the horror of the accident. We all have a story, you know. I wished I had a drink. Maybe two.

A while later, we turned into the drive that led to Brendan's and I looked to Sammy. "What are we doing here? I thought we were supposed to meet Brendan at your place."

"No need to go to my place. He wants us to meet him here—him and someone else."

The house came into view, the outline of Brendan's SUV barely visible in the fading light. Next to it was another vehicle. "Looks like Benny's here too, that's his new truck."

"What do you mean 'too'"?

Just then three figures walked down off the front porch. Straining to see, I noticed one in particular as they got closer. He was a bit thinner now, but when I saw the face, the smile was unmistakable—Paul.

I jumped from the Jeep and ran toward him. "Paul. What the heck are you doing here?" We hugged. "I mean... I thought you weren't able to make it out."

He wore a red Ohio State baseball hat. "You didn't think I'd miss seeing you out here, did you?"

"No, I guess not."

"Ah, there she is." Paul held out his arms. "The lovely Samantha Jane. How are you, my dear?"

"Just wonderful, Paul. And even better now that you're here." I watched them hug. I wonder why more people don't hug. I know we do it after a long absence, but why not more often? Like even after only a few days of not seeing someone special in our life?

The five of us settled onto the front porch. Brendan delivered a tray of cold beers and water. He stopped at Paul. "You allowed?"

"Yep, but just one. I've been looking forward to this little meeting for what seems like a long time."

We sipped our beers, and then Sammy spoke up. "So what's been going on, Paul? How are you? How about Maureen? And Becca and my friend Kate, that beautiful little girl?" *Still the same Sammy with her rapid fire questions.*

Paul sat back in his chair, crossing his legs. Even though it hadn't been a week since I'd last seen him, he looked much worse. The skin on his face was looser, and his pants were bunched at the waist.

"Oh, they're all fine. It's been great to really focus on all of them. They didn't want me to come out here, but I know deep down they understand why I did…why I had to."

Paul paused for a moment, looked at Benny, Sammy, me, finally resting his gaze on Brendan. "I have—at best—40, maybe 50 days left."

Canyon shifted his position lying there on the porch next to Brendan. I looked at Sammy who was looking at Brendan who was looking at Paul. We all seemed to retreat into our own space.

In my discomfort, I broke the silence. "Paul, are you sure about this? I mean isn't there anything the doctor—"

Paul interrupted, holding up his hand. His tone was peaceful and his face relaxed. "Jake, let's not spend our energy focused on this. I'm sick. My body will be stopping for good here in the near future. But right now I'm alive, and I want to focus on being alive. Do you remember we spoke about being alive, and the numbers of days Becca and I calculated?"

"I sure do. I'll always remember that. You said something like, 'And to me, there's one hell of a difference between living and being alive.'"

"Yes, I did. So let's focus on the fact that I'm not just living, I'm alive. I've been looking forward to coming out here to see all of you, especially you, Jake. Brendan asked me to spend some time with you tomorrow to help you continue your learning. Isn't that right, Brendan?"

Brendan turned from Paul to me. "What do you think?"

"Sounds good to me. I had a great chat with Vanessa today and I'm kind of thinking what she spoke about is one principle of Jackrabbit."

"Good. And you're right. We'll discuss that further, and what it means to you."

"Should I put the principle in the diagram?" I reached for my back pocket.

Brendan raised his brow. "What is it?"

"Well, I'm not really sure yet."

"Okay, then don't worry about completing the diagram right now, we can do it tomorrow morning. After that, you'll discuss another principle of Jackrabbit with Paul, and he's really good at practicing this one."

"You humble me, Brendan. And thanks for letting me chat with Jake, I'm anxious to dig into this topic. I think it'll help me as well, especially as I evolve with my sickness."

We engaged in some small chat with lots of laughs. Just before Sammy and Benny were getting ready to leave I turned to Benny.

"Benny, mind if I ask you a question?"

"You just did." He laughed and pointed at me as the others joined in. I could see why Benny had been so successful—or at least one reason why. Although he was a very big—and potentially intimidating—man, he had a very relaxed and easy manner. "Of course, Jake. What would you like to know?"

"Well, when I first met Paul in North Carolina a few weeks ago, he told me the story of how he first met Brendan. It was at a playground in Philly, during some pick-up basketball games. That true?" Benny nodded. "I ask because Paul said the story was so good I wouldn't believe it was true.

"Anyhow," I continued, "Paul told me that you were ready to haul off and punch some guy who made a wisecrack at you. But Brendan came up from behind and grabbed your arm before you could throw a punch. Is that how it happened?"

"Yep, that's what I remember." Benny leaned over, placing his beer bottle on the porch.

"Well," I glanced at Paul, who's smile suggested *go ahead, ask him.* "Why didn't you punch that guy? Or even Brendan for grabbing your arm?"

Brendan laughed. "Why didn't he punch me? Come on, don't give Benny any ideas here. I mean, I am trying to help you here. Is this how you show your appreciation?"

After some chuckles, Benny looked keenly at me. "Yes, that's how it happened, Jake, and here's what Brendan said to me. 'Hey Benny. I appreciate where you're coming from right now, that guy is a jerk and would probably benefit from you knocking him on his butt, but I kind of want to play on your team at some point here tonight. I like the way you play, you could help me with my game a bit, and how I get the ball inside to a strong big man. Here's the deal. If you crack this guy, I'm thinking the cops are gonna be here and the games will pretty much be over.'"

Benny stopped, and then looked to Brendan. "Then you said just two simple words that have stayed with me from that day on. You said, 'Your choice.'"

"I said that?"

"Absolutely." Benny looked quickly to Sammy and Paul, then back to me.

"Jake, it sounds weird that something so profound could happen from those simple words, but believe me when I tell you that being told that something was my choice was the first time in my life that I felt as though someone appreciated me, I mean really appreciated me. My parents were always working; they had to in order to raise me and my brothers and sisters. They loved me, but they were busy with life. Most girls liked me because I was big and muscular, and the guys either liked me because the girls did, or because they wanted to stay on my good side and not get their butt kicked. I'm not proud of it, but I wasn't such a nice guy back then.

"Then here comes this scrawny little guy not much older than I was, grabbing my arm and telling me he wanted to play on my team and that I had a choice in the matter." He motioned to Brendan. "I mean nobody ever grabbed me back then. He looks right into my eyes and makes me feel appreciated and valued. I'll never forget that. And let me tell you another thing—now that I'm on a roll." Benny winked. "My success, I mean our success as a company—and I'm continually humbled by it—is very dependent on our ability to make people feel appreciated. This is so key in business dealings. Many corporations would benefit from supporting their people in developing this skill—just how to appreciate others. Most folks focus on all the reasons to reprimand people instead of letting them know what they did—or what they do—well."

Benny paused. Then he spoke very seriously. "So that, Jake is why I didn't punch that guy—or Brendan for that matter—and why I'm thankful I've been friends with him for a long, long time."

I sat in silence along with the others, moved by the conviction with which Benny spoke.

Brendan broke the silence. "And I too am thankful I didn't get punched. I'd have wound up in another time zone. Thanks, Benny."

"Don't mention it." Benny winked again.

We exchanged our goodnights, and began to go our separate ways when Brendan grabbed my arm. "Jake, would you like to come stay at the bunkhouse now? Paul is staying here, too, so it will make it easier for you two tomorrow morning and I think you'd like it out here."

"Sure, Brendan. I'd like that. Thanks. But all my stuff is back at the motel."

"No problem," Sammy chimed in. "I'll drive you to the motel now and you can come right back here."

"Thanks, Sammy," Brendan said. Then he turned to me. "When you get back, just head to the bunkhouse over there"—he pointed to a long, low building—"and pick out any room you want. There's food and water in the refrigerator. Let's you and me meet first thing in the morning before you head out with Paul. I'd like to spend some time with you."

"Sounds good," I answered. He nodded and turned back to the house. "Sleep well."

I joined Sammy as she walked to her Jeep and we drove to my motel. When the car rolled to a stop in front of my motel, I grabbed the car door handle, but then released it and turned towards her. "Sammy, I wanted to thank you for today."

"For letting you paint?" She laughed.

"No. You know what I mean, for asking about my story—and for caring." I leaned in towards her, but she turned quickly and my kiss landed on the side of her head. She looked back to me after what seemed like a long time, her face serious.

"Jake, it was a good day, and I really enjoyed being with you and hearing your story. I appreciate you trusting me with it," she said. "But let's not complicate this. I like you and I know you like me, but we're just friends. Besides, your focus should be on getting better. I'll see you later."

Thankful for the darkness that I hoped hid my embarrassment, I got out of the Jeep and stood watching as the red lights bounced down the road.

17

An Uncomfortable Night

"The greatest griefs are those we cause ourselves."
–Sophocles

I packed quickly at the motel and drove out to Brendan's, hoping the truck's engine wouldn't disturb him as I parked in close to the bunkhouse. The night air was cool as I grabbed my bag and walked to the simple, front door. I went in and chose a small room at the front of the bunkhouse, dropping my bag as I explored the room. I grabbed a beer from my backpack— It wasn't vodka, but it would do—then lay down on the narrow bed. Tears came as I tried to run away from the pain caused from telling the story to Sammy a few hours earlier. I went back outside for a few minutes but the still night didn't help with my mood. I returned to the bed. My head ached as the film reel in my head played the same scene over and over: the feeling of Brian's lifeless lips on mine; his coarse mustache rubbing my finger as I pinched his nose and forced all the air from my lungs into his. His chest rising and falling. I did it again. And again. And again.

I wondered what Sammy was thinking about me trying to kiss her and hoped I hadn't ruined our friendship. I finished the beer, placed the bottle on the table, and realized I didn't have enough energy to get up and get another one.

Sometime later, I coughed a few times as the gas from the hose filled the small room. I coughed again, then nothing. The next thing I knew I was looking down at a police officer and a gray station wagon as the morning sun shined bright on the yellow tape hanging across the bunkhouse door. I watched two men slide a black bag into the back of the car. A man with the word CORONER on the back of his jacket shook his head slightly as he looked at the young officer. The back gate of the station wagon slammed just as I was going to speak to the cop.

I woke.

My breathing was fast—as if I'd just run a sprint—and my navy t-shirt was soaked. I shot up in bed, taking several deep breaths as I put my feet down on the cold, wooden floor. I got to the door quickly, gulping air as I opened it: no station wagon. Instead I was greeted by a full, silvery moon dripping eerie, gray light on everything. I saw Brendan's house, the SUV parked next to it. A hammock hung still between two small trees just off the front porch. I fell into the wooden chair on the small porch of the bunkhouse.

Man, that seemed so real. I thought I was gone. I have got to get past this… whatever this is. I placed my head back against the chair and stared into the star-filled sky.

With a sense of déjà vu, I felt the old thoughts taking over my brain. I have no idea what's going to happen and I'm scared. Brendan seems like a good guy, but who is he really, and why does he live out here in this canyon? What did he mean at Sammy's when he said he couldn't help me but I could help myself? And what—really—is this thing called Jackrabbit? Am I crazy to be here? Crap.

My head nodded, waking me and signaling it was time to return to bed. I tossed and turned until the first rays of sun peaked over the cliff and into the canyon. Specks of dust floating in rays of light hitting the floor were the first things I saw when I opened my eyes. Thank goodness, no more night.

18

Being Still With Myself

*"When one knows who they are
—who they really are—the path becomes clear."*

–Danny Bader

My mind raced, my head ached and I was tired. The back-pack caught my eye, but instead of grabbing a beer, I grabbed a pillow and tossed it on the floor, taking a seat cross-legged. I straightened my back, folded my hands lightly in my lap. *Try slowing down*, Vanessa had said. I closed my eyes, though it felt a bit weird to close them deliberately so soon after waking. But this was a different kind of closed. I began to focus on my breath. One, in, out. Two, in, out. The vision of the Coroner from my dream crept into my mind. I tried to banish it by pushing my brain in a new direction. I should call Mom today. I left Philly almost a week ago and haven't talked to her since I arrived.

I shook my head trying to chase these thoughts away. Darn, I need to clear my mind, focus on my breathing. Start over. One, in, out. Two, in, out. I think its working. Three, I wonder when I should go home; I mean how long will it take me to understand Jackrabbit. I marveled at how hard it was to just be quiet. Vanessa said I should let the thoughts flow in and then out very gently. Focus on my breath. Breathe. I took in a deep breath, let it out and rose to my feet.

This is going to take some discipline.

A few minutes later I found Brendan sitting on the worn leather chair in his small study with the window open. Sitting on his lap were several pieces of paper. He looked up as I entered. "Hello, Jake. All set for today?"

I thought about the dream I'd had, the first one where I actually saw the coroner's face, but decided not to bring it up. "Sure. I'm looking forward to it. What's on the agenda?"

"Well, a few things. First, I want to hear how your talk with Vanessa went. Then I'd like to spend some time exposing you to another of the Jackrabbit principles, and then you're off to spend time with Paul."

I nodded, settling into a wooden chair across from Brendan. Built-in bookshelves covered much of the wall space, and pictures filled in the rest. I glanced at one where I saw a younger Brendan with others holding surfboards at an ocean's edge. Their tan faces smiled and a dense, green jungle engulfed the picture behind them.

"So, about Vanessa, what'd you think?" he said. A few candles flickered around the study.

"This room is nice, kind of like a study."

"Yes, I love this space. I call it my book room. Actually, Vanessa comes here often to sit and read, or just to sit. Quite a few of these books are gifts from her, and many of the others are gifts as well."

I thought about the gifts I'd given over the years and realized not many were books. "Vanessa is a really cool lady. She's got something very peaceful about her, almost like you feel more relaxed just being around her."

"Yes, she's a remarkable woman. Maybe you can spend more time with her at some point—she's had a very fascinating life. Anything else?"

"Well, let me think. She talked a lot about really slowing down, kind of disconnecting from the busyness of our lives. I was really interested when she talked about the coaching she does with executives and how she won't work with people who aren't open to getting to a quiet place on a regular basis. And she makes a lot of money doing what she does."

"Yes, she does. And she does a lot of good with the money she makes from doing what she does." He winked.

I smiled, recalling my meeting with Benny and the yellow Lamborghini. "Yes, I remember. Money in and of itself is not good or bad, it's how one goes about getting it and what one does with it."

"I had a feeling you were going to be a fine student. Go on."

"It was also really cool how she hung out with the kids in that candlelit room. It looked weird at first, but then as I watched more, the kids looked so relaxed, so peaceful. When she and I were talking about me and my situation, I really liked one thing she said, I've been playing it over in my head, like a whisper: 'The action is the path.'"

He nodded.

"Yeah, she's cool. I liked chatting with her."

"Good, so last night you were right when you said you figured Vanessa spoke with you about a principle of Jackrabbit. What do believe it is?" Brendan inquired.

"I knew you were going to ask me that."

His eyes lit with enjoyment. "Good, then you should have an answer."

"I know I should and I've been thinking about it, and I've been coming up with some. But they seem too long, and confusing, or cliché." He nodded, raising his brow. "I know. I know what you're thinking. Like, 'make time every day to slow down, stop and smell the roses,' 'life's a rat race—you might win, but you're still a rat.'"

Brendan laughed out loud from deep in his belly and I couldn't help but join in.

"Brendan, you know what I'm talking about. People are always saying things like that. Countless t-shirts, bumper stickers and calendars are out there with these sayings. I know what they mean, but sometimes it just seems like too much. That said..."

"Yes?" Brendan prompted.

"This morning I actually tried applying what Vanessa talked about... you know, slowing down."

"How did that work for you?"

"Not very well." This time it was me who started the laughter.

"Don't sweat it, Jake," said Brendan. "Most of us have been trained from childhood to keep busy, to move fast when we move at all."

He took the papers from his lap, laid them on a small table next to him, and leaned forward a bit. "So, if you had to distill Vanessa's message down into two words, what would they be?"

I took a deep breath. "Hmm. She talked a lot about quiet, and disconnecting, and slowing down…"

Brendan nodded slowly. "Yes, and think back to what I just asked you, there's a clue in there."

I thought, but nothing came. "I don't know. You asked me what Vanessa talked about."

"No, I asked you to distill what she talked about down into two words. I asked you to distill…"

I held up my hand as Brendan overemphasized the syllable *still*. "I got it. Vanessa talked about stillness a lot."

"Yes." He rolled his hand. "And…"

"Well, she got the kids to be very still and she talked about the importance of executives, and all of us to be still."

He stood and gave me high five. "Bingo."

"Bingo what?" Then it hit me. "Be still."

Brendan leaned back in his chair and crossed his legs, wearing the same kind of smile I used to get from my fourth grade math teacher when I'd figured out a tough problem. I reached into my back pocket and pulled out the paper. I wrote the words *be still* in one of the four remaining spots, and then studied it for a moment. Canyon entered the room and plopped down next to Brendan's chair.

"Yes, be still. Do you understand it?"

I nodded. "In theory it makes great sense, but when I tried it this morning, I don't think it did much for me. I was trying to be still, but my mind kept racing. These ugly images crept in, then I started thinking about all the things I should be doing today. I didn't realize it would be that hard. I guess I can see how it might be helpful, but I don't know if I can do it."

"Don't give up so quickly, Jake. It takes time and discipline to be still. But trust me—you'll soon see the benefit. You saw what it did for the kids at the Center yesterday. But you'll need to make it a habit, like any change." He shifted in his chair. "So now that you have the first of the outer principles of Jackrabbit…" he pointed to the diagram I still held, "let's spend a little while talking about another one. We could probably spend about a week talking about it, but let me give you a quick overview. The principle is called know thyself."

I wrote those words down in another spot on my Jackrabbit diagram. "Know thyself… that sounds pretty simple, too, but I suspect maybe it's as hard in practice as being still!"

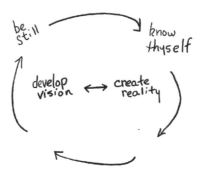

"This know thyself thing is what Socrates used to talk about." Brendan motioned to the other chair and I settled in. "It was actually inscribed at the temple of Apollo at Delphi. Socrates defined it this way when he wrote:

Know thyself; know your strengths and weaknesses;
your relation in the universe; your potentialities; your
spiritual heritage; your aims and purposes; take stock
of thyself.

I pointed to the papers on the table. "So what are those all about? Part of the lesson?"

"Ah, yes. I was reviewing them before you came in. They're my notes on know thyself." He took them off the table and pulled a paper from the small pile. "This is one my favorites, heck, they're all my favorites. This one's from one of the most interesting thinkers I've studied, Dr. William James, the grand-father of American psychology, who taught and researched at Harvard." Brendan read it out loud, slowly.

Seek out that particular attribute which makes you feel the most deeply and vitally alive, along with which comes the inner voice which says, 'This is the real me,' and when you have found that attitude, follow it.

He scanned down the page. "And another one. 'A happy life is one that is in accord with its own nature.' That's by the Roman philosopher, Seneca."

He laughed as he picked up a tiny sliver of paper, telling me it had come from a fortune cookie he opened after dinner in Ohio, where he was working with a large insurance company. '*Avoid unchallenging occupations—they will waste your great talents,*'" he read. "That's great advice...even if it did come from a cookie."

I laughed. Brendan uncrossed his legs and slid his glasses back to the top of his head.

"Think about all the folks that feel as though they're trapped in jobs and careers that they see as unchallenging in one way or another. Albert Camus wrote an essay about the Myth of Sisyphus, that Greek figure condemned by the gods to a life of futile and hopeless labor. He wrote, 'The workman of today works every day in his life at the same tasks, and this fate is no less absurd. But it is tragic only at the rare moments when it be-comes conscious.'"

I had read about that guy in high school and college. "He's the guy that rolled the stone up a hill, only to have it roll back down. Right?" Brendan nodded. "Then he had to do it again, and again. Yeah, I think I've seen a few people like Sisyphus out there."

"That's the guy. How true even today—and still tragic. I've seen quite a few myself." Brendan gave Canyon a rub under his chin, stood up and motioned toward the kitchen, where we stopped for another cup of coffee before settling on the front porch.

Brendan looked squarely at me. "Jake, do you know thyself? Tell me who you are."

I didn't really think about the question, I just started talking.

"What do you mean, who I am? You mean where I'm from? What I do for a living? How many brothers and sisters I have? What my mom and dad do for a living?"

"Maybe." He shrugged his shoulders. "Just tell me who you are. Pretend we don't know each other."

"I'm still not sure what you want to hear."

"That's what most people say. They try to anticipate what the other person wants to hear, whether that other person is a boss, a stranger at a party, a romantic interest, or the potential in-laws.

"Let's try this, Jake. Tell me how your best friend and your brothers would have described you had you died as a result of your accident."

"Wow, that's kind of morbid. I don't think I ever thought about that."

"Well, do you want to? Your choice. It's okay if you don't."

As I sipped my coffee, I peered over the rim of my mug, trying to figure out where he was going with this line of questioning. "Sure. My best friend would say that I loved life and was a good friend, one he could count on. He'd say I cared a lot about people and always tried to help where I could." I felt my shoulders tighten and my voice become strained. "My brothers would say I had good intentions but screwed up a lot. My girlfriend would say I'm afraid of commitment. How's that?"

"It's a start, but let's try to dig a little deeper. This principle of Jackrabbit is a very personal one. Many people I've coached, or who've contacted me after reading one of my books or hearing me speak, have had some powerful observations about their journey to know thyself, and how what they discover about themselves is not aligned with the way their life is at the moment. What we're discussing here is very much connected to what Thoreau meant when he said, 'The mass of men lead lives of quiet desperation.'"

"Did these people come to see things—thyself—differently?"

"Great question, Jake, you touched on the key point of this principle."

"I did?"

"Absolutely. The people didn't see themselves—thyself, as you put it—differently. They had the courage to look deep inside and see themselves as they are. They only call it seeing themselves 'differently' because too often people go through life numb to who they really are, and lead lives where they are not themselves."

Brendan explained that people often think of "who they are in this world" based on their relationships and achievements... the money they make or don't make, the houses they live in or don't live in, or the positions they hold or don't hold in society and organizations. He continued, "What's key is that they're not really any of those things. Who and what people think they *should* be has led them to all of these things and places. If all of this—material things, where they live, how they live, what they do to earn a living—is truly connected to who they really are, then they likely haven't done the work needed to know themselves deeply. When people really connect with the disconnect of where they are in relation to where they want to be, then they make some significant and liberating changes."

"You're losing me." I shook my head, placing my mug on the railing. I shoved my hands into my pockets. "Is knowing thyself a part of the develop vision, create reality principle we discussed?" We stood opposite one another on the porch, each of us leaning back against the railing. Brendan's legs crossed at the ankles, his old boots one atop the other.

"Sure. How can one develop a vision and move to action to create that vision when they're not sure who they are, or worse yet perhaps avoiding who they really are? A lot of folks develop a vision and turn it into reality, only to be miserable and unfulfilled. I worked once with a young guy, a real nice young guy that was in sales. He was in sales because everybody close to him thought he'd be good at it. 'After all', they said, 'you're intelligent, well-spoken, a good communicator, and you present yourself well.'"

I shrugged. "He sure sounds like someone who would enjoy sales."

"The problem, Jake, is he hated it. He didn't like all the rejection that occurs in sales. He didn't like the introverted time that comes with a sales position. He was by himself much of each day driving between clients and completing reports and proposals, and this was a major drain on his energy. Plus — and probably most importantly — he just didn't see himself as a salesperson."

Brendan glanced to the bunkhouse, rubbing his stubble chin. "I just read a great quote a few minutes ago by Seneca, 'A happy life is one that is in accord with its own nature.' Remember that one?" I nodded. "You see, Jake, it wasn't in this young man's nature to be a salesperson. During our coaching relationship he said many times that he hated to tell people what he did, it was like he was telling a lie. It was a lie for him because he'd not developed his vision. He told me many times that he had settled."

"Settled?"

"Yes, you know, when someone makes a choice to live somewhere, work somewhere, enter into or stay in a relationship, do something—or not do something—that deep in their gut they know isn't the best choice for them. They settle."

My chest rose as I took in a very deep breath. "Yes I've seen that… actually done it myself a bit. So knowing thyself has to do with what you do for a living?"

Brendan glanced toward the trail up the canyon, then back to me. "Well, yes…sometimes … and no, in all the other times. Knowing thyself has to do with a lot."

"This should be interesting." I moved from my leaning position to the chair in the corner.

Brendan ran his hands through his long, grey hair, and then clasped them behind his head, smiling at my sarcasm. "Yes, yes it is. Knowing thyself—to me, as a principle of Jackrabbit—is about a person striving to get into the rhythm of their life, and this rhythm is dynamic. To know thyself is definitely about the strengths and weaknesses we possess as individuals. You know, are we good with people, how do we communicate, how do we analyze data, do we like structure or spontaneity? Are we more comfortable with the ways things are? Or more driven and energized by seeking ways to make things different? Do we have the talent for seeing things in a different light? Do we prefer to work at a large company? Or a small one? Are we living in the right part of the country? State? Town?"

"Kind of like what you get from those personality tests and assessments. You know, 'Am I a dolphin or a lion?'"

"Sure, you know what I mean." Brendan kicked a small pebble off the porch. "And by the way, I'd say you are a dolphin if I had to guess. You seem to me, that prior to the accident, you liked to have fun, and explore new things and be creative—some of the characteristics of the dolphin type."

"Yep," I laughed. "That's me, Jake the dolphin, although I don't feel like one right now."

"Well, there are quite a few assessments and instruments that I believe can help people identify their innate strengths and likes. I'll usually suggest people complete one or two."

"Makes sense. I could probably use some of these, considering where I am now."

"Yes, you'll want to engage with a few. I think it will definitely help with the professional side of your vision. These characteristics or traits are all worldly things, those things of the body and brain, how we engage with the world, and the information and communication all around us. But there's another side—to me a more inherent and mysterious side—of knowing thyself that has to do with a person's spiritual side, their soul, and I don't believe we can get to that through an assessment. Remember in the inscription Socrates mentioned, 'your spiritual heritage.' To get to this point I believe it's vital for people to set aside time to be still."

I nodded. "Is that why your design is circular with the arrows going to the middle of the diagram, to vision and reality, and then back out again? There seems to be a real easy flow between the principles, kind of like the rhythm you just mentioned."

"Yes, these principles are entwined, and folks tell me they're better when they spend time with them all, in a constant and continuous manner." Brendan moved his hand in slow circles in front of him. "You, for instance, may need to *be still* more than me at this point because you need to work on your vision.

Remember, it's often in the absence of sound that we hear the most. I, on the other hand, have a pretty clear vision. I need to work on some of the other principles more."

"Yeah, I'm thinking I need to do some work with this principle of knowing myself as well."

"Probably a good idea." Canyon rose from his napping spot and made his way off the porch toward the bunkhouse.

Brendan sat next to me, looking deep into my eyes. "Jake, it's being able to say 'this is who I am.' It does help to know thyself in the worldly sense—being able to say 'this is what I do and why I like doing it.' But we must always remember we are not what we do. Rather, we are *how* we do what we do."

"Now you're losing me again, Brendan."

"Yes, sorry. Here's how it kind of hit me. I've been a speaker for many years and I've been told I'm a very good speaker because I really know my subject and have a lot of experience, I know how to deliver a speech well with good timing, I have a good vocabulary, a nice, strong voice, and so on. I'm humbled and thankful when people comment on things like that, but those are superficial abilities. It took me some time to know myself in the worldly sense, to know that I *liked* speaking, and the research and travel that came with it—at least most times. To know that I hate routine, and love meeting a lot of new people almost every week, and having the chance to help them learn and grow. My success as a speaker and coach has also provided me the opportunity to live here, in the desert. I've tried city life, but it's just not a good fit for me. Anyhow, I began to speak more and I think I was pretty good at it."

"Okay, that makes sense. You were applying your worldly strengths."

"Yes, but there's more. It wasn't until I got to know myself spiritually, my soul, that I really understood the power of this principle. For many years I was a speaker, and I must admit I loved all the accolades I received. It was good for my ego. But then it clicked for me and I realized that myself, my soul, was love. Period." He paused, glancing to the sky.

"You see, Jake, I realized I'm on this earth to Love, and that was it. I wanted to spend each day caring for others, striving to help them help themselves to become better people, striving to leave this world a little better because I've lived. I'm not sure when I realized this. It wasn't the bolt of lightning thing. Although, I had a good jolt of this realization once on a beach in Costa Rica. And I know I'm not finished."

I let Brendan's words settle in, replaying them back a few times. "Sounds like the way Jesus lived."

"Sure does, doesn't it? You're right. I reread the four gospels, and a bunch of other books. I began every day to strive to emulate the ways of Jesus, and some other great spiritual people from history. This is not an easy thing to do. I've failed often — still do — but it's wonderful to try again each day. So, just as Jesus was the purest form of Love, I began to see myself — to know myself as a loving person who happened to be a speaker. Then — and this is the point I'm making, Jake — I believe I became a great speaker. I believe we're all this Love. Haven't you ever just felt God in someone?"

I nodded slowly, not looking at Brendan.

"And this isn't just my experience, but that of thousands of others I've known over the years. They told me when they understood this dimension of knowing thyself, then they became great moms and dads, teachers, plumbers, nurses, business owners, bartenders, golf pros, doctors, toll booth operators or whatever they did in this world. After all, most of us need to work to provide for ourselves and families."

"I was in the presence of this Love you talk about. I call it God," I said quietly.

"Yes, I know you were, Jake. I believe that you still are. That we all are." Brendan spoke as quietly as me.

"Continue exploring and working with this principle, Jake. You'll be glad you did. It's vital to really know yourself so as to develop a strong vision, and it's also very connected to one's purpose. It will likely even help you make some sense of your dream. In all that you do, both personally and professionally — try to lead with love. You see it's not so much what we do, but the process by which we go about the doing. Money, houses, material things are wonderful, so long as the person knows thyself and pays particular attention to how they go about getting the money and house, and how the house and everything else is reflective of our authentic self. Buddha once said, 'Your work is to discover your work and then with all your heart give yourself to it.' So, in summary, strive always to know thyself, and then be thyself."

I stood up to join him. "Hmm, sounds a lot like something I remember from studying St. Francis de Sales in college. He wrote, 'Strive to be nothing other than what you are, and be that perfectly.'"

"Exactly, that's it," said Brendan. "Good conversation. I saw you filled this principle in on your paper, be sure to begin focusing on it."

I looked at the increasingly crumpled paper in my hands. "These words are so simple, but they represent some very complicated principles."

"I did that on purpose, Jake. One thing people tell me they love about Jackrabbit is its simplicity — it's easy for them to remember. But within that simplicity is an ever-present invitation to explore more deeply. I found that the simpler the model — the framework—the easier it is to get into it. And that's where the good work lies. I think some folks overcomplicate the message they're trying to deliver. It's almost like they believe the more complex their idea or theory, the more attractive it will be to folks. I'm sure much of it is great work, but for me much of it's too complicated."

"Couldn't agree more," I said.

"Good. Although truth be told, I get nervous when someone meets me and asks 'What else is there I should be thinking about? I read your book and enjoyed it. I think I've got Jackrabbit.' I get nervous because I don't believe anyone ever 'gets it.' I've been working with this philosophy for over thirty years, and I absolutely know I haven't 'got it.' I want you to understand that Jackrabbit is a guide for our journey, it's not a course you complete."

Brendan stood and held out his hand to me. "Enough of the preaching for today! I think you're off with Paul here this morning. Have fun."

"Oh, I will."

He opened the door to the house.

I called after him. "And Brendan," I said as he turned towards me, "thanks."

"You're welcome."

The door closed behind Brendan. What a special man. I walked toward the bunkhouse as another thought popped into my head; Faith, Hope and Love, and the greatest of these is Love.

19

Getting Unstuck

"Press on."

—St. Paul

I went to the bunkhouse and put my shoes on, dropped my hat on backwards then walked back to the main house. Upon entering the kitchen I was greeted with a lick on the hand by Canyon. Paul sat with a cup of coffee and a bowl of cereal in front of him. "Good morning." His smile felt warm and familiar by now. "Hungry?"

"Sure am. Let me grab some toast and then we can get started. Are we going someplace today?" I did my best to put on a happy face after my talk with Brendan, but the residue of my dream was still thick.

"Well, I figure we could take the bikes and go for a ride before it gets too hot. I may have to rest and walk a bit."

"Sure you can handle that, Paul? I don't want you to tire yourself out just for me."

"I think a ride will be good for me."

"OK, if you say so. It sounds great." I popped the toaster down.

Brendan walked into the room. "Hey, guys. How are you doing this morning, Paul?"

"Doin' good." Paul wore a long sleeve t-shirt with khakis. "We're going to ride our bikes to the back ridge."

"Sounds like fun." Brendan turned to me. "Do you think you could walk me to my car? I'm off for a few days to do some work with a fellow back your way in Philly, and I wanted to chat about one more thing."

I grabbed my toast, spread some peanut butter on it, and watched as Brendan gave Paul a quick handshake that turned into a hug and said he'd see him in few days.

As we walked out the front door, I mumbled to Brendan through the peanut butter and toast. "You're going away?"

"Yep, just a few days. I'm hoping you'll stay here and feed Canyon for me... and maybe have a few more conversations with people I think can help you. Deal?"

"Deal," I replied quickly.

"Good chat this morning," Brendan continued. "Thanks for your time. Before I left, I wanted to touch base to see how you're doing. I've had you working pretty hard since you came.

"I know by that paper in your back pocket that you pulled out earlier that you're taking this Jackrabbit idea seriously. And that you're struggling now to develop your vision and think about what it will take to create a new reality for yourself. You learned about being still with Vanessa, and this morning we talked about 'know thyself'—the foundation for living a truly authentic life, to live on purpose. And there's still more I'd like you to learn, starting with your time with Paul today. But it's important for people to go at their own pace. So here's my question—How are you?"

I responded quickly. "Brendan, I was thinking it's been great for me to get away and come out here, and I've really learned a lot in just a few days. I feel like I should be healing already, but truth be told… at the moment I don't feel so good."

Brendan said nothing, just shifting his head a little to the side as to say "go on."

I swallowed, and then went on. "I had a dream last night that I ran a hose from my truck's tailpipe into my room and went for a long, long sleep."

"Hmm, that must have been disturbing." His eyes locked into mine. "Can I take it from your reaction that you've had that dream before?"

"I used to have them frequently. Last night's was the worst since I've been here. That's why I don't feel so good."

"I can imagine how hard it would be to have that kind of dream. Do you think there's a reason why you had it?"

"I'm… I'm not sure," I replied. "I thought they'd stopped, but I don't know, maybe it is the new environment, the change. Once before I thought I was getting better, then something happened to remind me that my friend Brian died and I lived. It seems like something is telling me I can't get past this. Yesterday, I told Sammy about what really happened in my accident. I think I said more to her than I have to any other person, including my family. In some way, I thought that talking about it would make some of the pain go away. But it hasn't."

I glanced away, and then looked directly into Brendan's eyes. "Brendan, I don't want to stop living anymore. I want to be *here* and engaged with life. I want to get better. All the people I've met that seem to be living by your principles seem happy and fulfilled, even though Sammy told me recently that she may need to develop a new vision that involves moving on from here. Some have lots of money, some don't. Some are healthy, some are facing health challenges. Some are old, some are young. A part of me thinks that if I can apply your Jackrabbit principles I'll be okay, but I'm not sure. Another part of me—the deep part of my brain that's in charge of the dreams—knows that nothing has really changed yet. Surrounded by you and Sammy and Paul, I'm hanging in there. But deep down, I'm afraid that as soon as I leave here it will all go back to the way it's been. It's like this part of me doesn't want to get better."

Brendan drew a deep breath then exhaled. "Two things, Jake. One, I'm humbled when you say the principles are mine. It's true that I bundled these principles, and named the approach to living them 'Jackrabbit,' but these principles have been around for many, many years. It's been through my own observations, and through working with different people that I came to realize that when these particular principles are done in unison, consistently, completely..." he paused, "...that people become happier and more fulfilled."

"Two, you just mentioned that if you apply these principles you'll be okay. Jake, you have begun to apply them. You went through an experience that was both horrible and profound at the same time. It's not unusual for it to take a long time to work through that. For what it's worth, I think you are healing. I've worked with a lot of people, and I can tell you that it's a very positive sign that you're open to having new experiences and accepting people for who they are, to exploring who you are and what you are. It's not easy work, and the fact that you're still here tells me a lot about your character."

"Do you really mean that?"

"Of course I do, Jake. I'm certain you've applied some—if not all—of these principles before you met Paul and me, and before your accident. What I've seen is that many people wait until the world beats them up enough and then they're kind of forced to apply some of Jackrabbit. Or deal with the consequences."

"Consequences?"

"That's right. People go on and experience no change. They don't move toward a new vision. Most have never had one to begin with. They stay in the same nasty job, stale relationship, state of health, and/or wealth, and on and on and on. They suffer the brutal consequences of staying where they do not want to be." Brendan stopped talking, looked off beyond the hood of his SUV and shook his head slowly. He turned back to me, the morning sun reflecting all around us.

"Jake, don't focus on it. You have to see yourself living this way. You can easily change your thinking and behavior to reflect these principles. Trust me. It's not as difficult as folks make it out to be. Some are just so conditioned to complaining and blaming everyone and everything that they stay stuck."

"Right, we get what we focus on."

"Exactly." Brendan gave me a hug. "See you in a few days. Be well."

That was the first time he hugged me. It felt good. "You too." As he climbed into the SUV, I called after him. "Say, Brendan... would it be OK if I jump in the hot tub tomorrow morning? I don't think I'll have time today, but I thought it would be nice to jump in tomorrow morning and watch the sun come up."

"Sure thing," he called back. "Use it any time." His SUV drove down the winding road.

I went back inside, finished my breakfast, cleaned my dishes and walked outside. Paul stood, holding out a small backpack to me. "I packed some granola bars and fruit, but you are going to have to carry this. It's gonna be too much for me."

"Sure thing." I swung the pack across my shoulders.

We grabbed our bikes and started up the rocky dirt trail behind the house. The sun peeked over the horizon, its rays not yet warming the morning air. Deep breaths of cool air helped me relax.

Paul took the lead, pedals churning at a quick pace. Remarkable, the man's dying and look at him go. I guess we can generate some power with the right thinking!

"You're looking pretty good up there, Paul."

"Yeah, there's something about the desert, and being out here with you and the others that seems to give me a lift. Let's go a little farther. I want you to see something."

We rode on until Paul slowed, got off his bike, and laid it on the slick rock. The ride had not been steep, but the tightness in my thighs and quick breathing confirmed that it was definitely all uphill.

Paul turned to me. "Let's walk up to the end of this ridge."

I followed the old man, the back of his neck shiny with sweat. After walking about half a football field, we sat down on a rock, both of us just paces from the edge of a cliff.

He pointed across the deep canyon in front of us. "There it is. That's what I wanted you to see."

Peering over the edge, I recognized the highway hugging the river below. It was the road I'd traveled into Moab. I followed Paul's gaze to the other side and grinned as my eyes stopped on a large hole in the rock wall high above the water. It was the one I'd seen when I had pulled over for a rest. It looked different from this angle, but there was no mistaking the unique, almost perfect circle.

"Now how did that hole get like that? You know, Paul, it's kind of funny that you're showing me this. I stopped by the river on my way into Moab because I was really nervous about meeting Brendan and I needed a break. I was wondering about it and made a mental note to ask Brendan about it."

Paul nodded as he gazed across. "Sure is something, isn't it? It took a long, long time for it to get that way. You probably know, Jake, that Brendan asked me to get with you today to chat some more about Jackrabbit."

I nodded.

"What does the word evolve mean to you?"

I thought for a moment. "I guess I think of the word evolve, or evolution, and how the world keeps changing."

"Good, good. Right in line with the definition I like.... 'to undergo continuous and gradual change.' Man, this is a very important part of Jackrabbit, this notion of change. I mean all the principles are important, but this one's been instrumental in my life, especially over the past decade or so. I think that's why Brendan asked me to introduce it to you."

"So you've been evolving?"

"Very much so. When Brendan and I first discussed Jackrabbit a long time ago, he said, 'Paul, if you were to go to sleep tonight knowing that you won't wake in the morning, would you be content with how you spent today? Where you directed your focus?' I remember it well." He shook his head and stared out over the river.

"We were out on a ride and stopped by a stream to water our horses. I didn't know what to say, so I told him I needed to think it over. I handed him the reins to my horse then walked upstream a ways. And as I walked I thought about the day and what I'd done. The calls I'd made earlier in the day, the reading and a hike I'd taken. But I didn't stop there. I began to think about the past week, the past month... year... decade. I know now that Brendan's question wasn't asked so much to get me thinking about the day, but rather about how I'd lived up to that point. He was asking me if I was comfortable, content...fulfilled is the word I'm looking for. He was asking if I was fulfilled with everything that I'd achieved up to that point in my life."

I grabbed the water bottles from the backpack, handing one to Paul. "So what'd you say?"

Paul laughed, rubbing his head. "Well, I stayed away for about 20 minutes. I was really trying hard to think of something profound to say to Brendan. You ever been there? You know, when you're thinking about being clever, or smart and sophisticated, as opposed to just thinking?"

I nodded. "Oh, yeah, I've been there a bunch of times. Well, what'd you say? Come on, Paul, the suspense is killing me."

Paul broke into a slight grin. "No."

"No? No what?"

"After coming up with nothing profound and philosophical to say, I walked back to Brendan and said 'No.' He looked back at me with a smile and said, 'Good. Tell me what it—your day today—would've looked like if you'd been able to say yes.'

"I thought for a moment and said that I guess I would have spent the day focused on the most important things I need to be focused on. Brendan asked me, 'How do you define important?' I said that it was the things that needed to get done, my priorities. 'And what *are* your priorities? Your work?' he asked. That man can ask some questions."

"You can say that again."

Paul took a swig of water. "Well, I guess work things were very important, at least they looked that way back then. Don't know that I'd give a rat's ass about any work stuff right now, I mean, if I was still working. What Brendan helped me start understanding is that many of us need to become more aware of where we're putting—and maybe more importantly—not putting our focus. It's easy to lose sight of what's important because most people hit the ground running every day. They run hard all day long and at the end of the day they're exhausted. Then they do it again and again and again. And you want to know what the sad thing is?"

"What?"

"These folks... and I was one of them... will tell you they are always tired. But that a huge majority of them ... myself included... can't even verbalize what they're tired about. They have no idea how they are spending their precious focus."

We sat in silence, staring at the hole in the rock across the river.

"You know, Jake, it's the experiences we have throughout our life that make us whole, even when some of these experiences leave holes in us, like that rock over there. Would you agree?"

"I guess. I mean, I guess we're a product of our experiences."

"Close, my young friend, but ponder this. Maybe we're not the product of our experiences, but rather the product of what we learned from our experiences—the good and the not so good. 'The fool is a fool because he doesn't know how to learn from his experience. The wise man is wise because he does.' Gallwey. The Inner Game of Tennis. Heard of it?"

I shook my head, and then chuckled a bit. "Hmm, I guess I've been a fool many times over—without even playing tennis."

"Yeah, me too." Paul grinned at me. "But not so much since I began to think about what Gallwey is saying, which isn't just about tennis. Rather, how have we changed our thoughts about what has happened to us over time? In short, how have we—and *are* we evolving?" Paul looked intently at me, then across to the hole. "Every gust of wind and every drop of rain makes that hole over there a little different. Its shape is the sum of all its experiences. It's the same with us." He paused. "You getting this?"

I smiled reflectively. "Yeah. Yeah. I'm getting this."

"You'll do well to spend some time thinking not so much about what happened to you, but what you've learned so far," said Paul. "And think about what you'll continue to learn from what happened to you. And how this learning will change you — how you'll evolve."

We sat for several moments, watching the tiny cars wind across the desert floor. After another drink of water, we jumped on the bikes and cruised back to the house. I leaned my bike against the porch. He waited for me. "I think I'm going to lie down. I'm pooped, but I'm glad I got to speak with you." He stepped up onto the porch and reached for the screen door.

"Hey, Paul." He turned. "Me too. Thanks. I know it was a huge effort for you to come all the way to Utah. And I really appreciate your time… not just here, but in North Carolina, too."

"It's been my pleasure, Jake." He started going through the door.

"Hey, Paul," I called after him. "What's this principle called?"

Holding the door half-open, he pointed at his feet and slowly up his body, stopping at his head. "Evolve." He winked and disappeared.

Right, I said to myself. I pulled the paper from my back pocket, scrounged up the marker from another pocket, and wrote "Evolve" in another spot of the diagram.

20

Chillaxin'

"If you are going through Hell, keep going."
—Winston Churchill

After a quick shower I drove over to Tuscany. Entering the center I saw the little girl that was with Vanessa the day I met her. She was curled up on the cushioned window seat in the lobby, a colorful blanket around her shoulders. Man, what's her name? Sandy, Susie? I took a deep breath and relaxed. It came. Sophie. Yes, Sophie, that's it.

I walked to her. "Hi, Sophie. How ya doing today?"

Her eyes looked up and over the book she was reading. A mermaid and sea witch stared at me from the cover.

"Hi." She laid the book down next to her.

"Good book?"

"It's okay. I already read it a hundred times."

"A hundred times? Wow, you must really like it."

"Yeah, it's okay, but mostly I just like to come here and sit in this window. The sun feels good."

"Well, you do look comfy. Hey, Sophie, have you seen Noah today?"

She bit her lower lip and scrunched up her nose, wrinkles forming beneath her curly bangs. "Yep, he was around a few minutes ago. He's probably in the kitchen looking for something to eat again. He eats a lot."

"Thanks, Soph. See you again I hope."

"Sure. Look for me right here."

I walked a few hallways, then turned a corner and entered the kitchen. Noah was parked at the far window. He sat still, staring toward the mountains in the distance.

"Hey, Noah, what's up?"

The boy turned to me, an orange sports drink in his hand. "Well, well, well. The master painter returns."

"Yes. Indeed, that's me. How's it look? Did it dry alright?"

He grinned. "Better than I thought it would. Maybe if you keep going and do the rest of the center, you'll actually become decent."

"What are you doing over here all alone?"

"Just chillaxin'."

"Mind if I join you?"

"I'll let you stay under one condition," Noah quipped.

"And what might that be?"

"Can I see your scars? I've never known anyone who was electrocuted before."

"My scars? Who told you I had scars?" I was playing for time, not sure how to respond. No one had ever asked me that question before.

"I don't remember, I just heard some of the big people talking and they said that, like, a million volts of electricity went through you and you had these big gaping holes in your feet."

"Well..." I wasn't sure how I felt about this. I hated looking at the scars because of all the reminders they carried with them.

"I guess if you don't want to, it's OK. You know I get to see all sorts of things here and in the hospital... but I've never seen holes burnt into anyone's feet before..."

Suddenly I found myself laughing. "They aren't exactly holes anymore," I said. "And it wasn't a million volts. But if you really want to see them, I guess it's alright."

And that's how, for the first time since the accident, I found myself deliberately taking off my socks and shoes to show off my scars. And then for the next fifteen minutes, I actually enjoyed having an intelligent conversation with a 10 year old boy about what it's like to get hit by electricity. The ghosts were still there, but they stayed in the shadows.

Afterwards, we sat for a moment longer and then I turned. "OK, now it's my turn, Noah. Can I ask you a question?"

"Sure."

"You being sick and all, what do you think about it?"

He turned to me, his eyes questioning. "Why do you want to know?"

"I don't know, really. I was just talking with Paul this morning..."

"He's sick too, you know. He told me. We've talked a lot."

"Yeah, I know. He's been telling me a little of what he's learned from being sick. I guess I was just wondering what you think about…" I paused as my stomach tightened and the little voice in my head screamed, *stop*, "…about you being sick."

Noah smiled for a moment and then got very serious. "Okay, Jake, since you asked, here it is. Here's what I think, the way I look at it. This sucks. In fact, it's a major pain in my ass. And don't tell my mom and dad I used that word."

I smiled back at him, raising my hand. "I won't. I promise."

"I don't want to be here, and I can think of a million places I'd rather be. Like at home, at school, or with my friends. But when I think about getting better, and what it'll be like when I'm better, it's good. It's good for me, it's good for my mom and dad, sister and brother, my friends, my teachers, for everyone… it's just good. It kind of reminds me of Tigger—from Winnie the Pooh." He paused and looked at me to see if I knew the reference.

"Tigger, right. The Tigger."

"I remember from the books my mom read to me that Tigger was always happy and having a good time—all the time. I wanted to be like that, to be happy all the time."

I squashed my urge to challenge him with the impossibility of that goal, but realized he probably knew better than anyone how hard it was to be happy all the time. If he could try to be happy, certainly I could, too. So I just said, "Yeah, I should probably read all those children's books again. There seems to be a lot of great lessons in them."

He paused for some time, I can't say exactly how long. For me, periods of silence always last longer in tough conversations.

"Jake, you adults say things like this all the time to me to make me feel better. And I can tell that sometimes people don't believe it. But I *will* get better. I will be healthy soon. One thing I've learned is this is not forever, nothing is."

A feeling engulfed me that I'd never experienced before. I felt thankful, scared, confused, and hopeful—very hopeful—all at the same time. Very weird.

I saw in this young boy's eyes a sense of true belief that I know I'd never seen in anyone's eyes before, and a chill ran through my body. "Thanks, Noah. I'll see you around."

"You can count on it, hot-shot." He gave me five as he wheeled around and rolled away.

I remember feeling like I wanted to talk more with Noah, but didn't know what to say.

Churchill once said, "If you are going through Hell, keep going." Yeah, he's going through hell all right, and that brave little dude is gonna keep going. *This Evolve thing is huge. I don't think I ever thought about it this way. The challenges, the experience, that Noah is facing will change him forever, change him for the better. This has got to be making him a stronger kid because of the way he's thinking about it. I thought evolution, to evolve, to undergo gradual and continuous change was for dinosaurs, and planets, and species over thousands and millions of years. Our opportunity to evolve happens every day—with every experience. I gotta remember this.*

I went to sleep that night in a more peaceful state than I'd experienced in a long time—a very long time.

21

Anything But Alone

"Too many people attempt to go it alone in this world, when they are anything but alone."

–Danny Bader

Early the next morning I rolled out of bed onto my knees for what I was determined to make a daily ritual: making the first few moments of each new day a time to be still—a time to pray. The soreness in my calves and thighs distracted me from prayer, reminding me of the bike ride with Paul. I finished my prayers then pulled on my trunks, slid into my sandals and t-shirt and opened the door, shivering as the morning air hit me. The sky was clear, stars fading into a barely lit horizon. The desert was still. No traces or sounds of wildlife. I made my way behind Brendan's house and started up the trail. Approaching the hot tub, I smelled burning wood. It reminded me of the days when my dad would roll up newspapers in the fireplace to start the kindling burning and get the flue draft going.

I followed the path between two bushes. The smoke caused me to squint as I rounded a bend and the hot tub came into view. It wasn't a traditional hot-tub—the fiberglass kind with jets. Instead, it was a large cistern that had been cut in half and placed into the side of the hill. The right side was level with a large boulder protruding from the slope, the left was propped on stones and blocks that raised it to about three feet off the ground.

Stones underneath formed a circle about four feet across. In the middle coals glowed. Brilliant. How cool is that? I stopped. Not more than ten steps away hung a huge tattooed arm over the side of the tub. I instantly recognized the Virgin Mary, the one I'd seen in my first two minutes at Sammy's place just a few days ago.

Oh no! You've got to be kidding me. Preacher? What the hell's he doing here at six in the morning? I can't stay now; I wonder if he saw me? No, there's no way. He looks like he's asleep. I can just turn slowly and quietly and …..

"Well. Good morning, Jake." His voice was deep and gruff, a blend of cigarettes and too much whiskey. "I was wondering when you'd show up."

I said nothing. I was frozen.

"You thinkin' about leaving before we even get a chance to talk?"

"No, no.… I mean I don't want to interrupt you or anything. I can come back later."

Preacher turned around and leaned on his crossed arms as I made my way slowly toward the tub. I think he smiled, but I wasn't really watching his face. All I could see were tattoos—a lot of them.

"Jake, Jake, Jake. You're not interrupting me. It's because of you that I'm here. Come get your butt into this hot tub so we can get started."

I shifted my weight. "Get started?"

"Yeah, with our lesson. Brendan told me you were gonna watch the sun rise from the hot tub. Don't mind sayin' I think that's a great idea, I been meanin' to get over here myself. Brendan also asked If I could talk with you about the final principle of Jackrabbit. How lucky are you my man? To get the final principle of Jackrabbit from the Preacher." He laughed to himself.

I'd noticed last night that there was only one blank spot left on my diagram. "You know about Jackrabbit?" I managed to say.

"Sure do. Lookin' at me now, I'm sure you can see that I'm all sweetness and light." He grinned at me in a way that I wouldn't call either sweet or light. "But I've been through some stuff. And from what I hear, you have been too.... But I don't really know what brought you to Moab. You lookin' for something? Some kind of support group, maybe? I don't do support groups." He turned around and rested his head back on the lip of the tub.

I climbed up the side of the hill and dipped a foot into the steaming water. I wouldn't have pegged him as the support group type, either. "Um. Well, I guess so. I mean I was going nowhere on my own... um, at least nowhere good. So I guess I did come here looking for some support. Seems like most people need some support from time to time."

"Sure we do. Life can throw us some nasty crap. It beats the bejesus out of us. That's what makes it so fun." He paused briefly before continuing. "So where do you get yours from?"

"Get what?" The water was hot, almost boiling. I thought of that old cartoon where natives with bones through their noses are surrounding a pot of boiling tourists. I felt like those tourists.

Preacher cupped his hands, scooping up some water to splash on his face and slick his hair back. "What I mean is, do you got anybody in your life… you know, like to talk to. It was obvious to me—as soon as I saw you in Sammy's—that you were pretty f…f…f… screwed up. You kind of seemed to me like a loser. You be sure to tell Brendan I said screwed up instead of the other word." Preacher grinned. "I'm cleaning up my language."

I was pissed at this guy, but punching Preacher wasn't an option. I wasn't that suicidal. "What do you mean by screwed up? We didn't talk at all in Sammy's… but it sure looked like you wanted to kick my butt that day. Maybe you're the one who's screwed up."

Preacher grimaced—at least I think it was a grimace. "Oh, man, I'm sorry. I was just in a bad mood that day…well, had been for a while."

I wasn't sure how to react. Hearing an apology from Preacher was the last thing I'd expected, and I was lost for words. I tried to think about what Brendan would do or say. "I don't know what I can do, but if you need any help…"

Preacher laughed so hard the water splashed out of the hot tub. "Thanks, Jake, but I'm doing better now. Maybe you got this notion that it's going to be smooth sailing from now on… from hanging out with people like Brendan and Paul and Vanessa. But that ain't the way it is. I think we're all screwed up, most of the time."

"That seems a little harsh."

"Don't mean it to be. I just mean that most people's lives aren't the way they want them to be. You know what Brendan talks about with his reality and vision thing." I nodded. "You're never going to find that perfect balance."

I wanted to punch him again for criticizing Brendan's model. But fear and curiosity won out. "Do you mean Brendan's wrong?" I asked.

"No, man. I'm not dissin' Brendan. I just mean that once you create the reality you want, then that vision's done. It's not doin' anything for you anymore. And the way I see it, that's a good time to think about a new vision." He paused, and then scrutinized me. "Or maybe not. Maybe you're one of those people who wants to stay where they are for a stretch." Preacher turned his head to rest it again on the rim of the hot tub, and closed his eyes. "I just hope they don't want to stay there forever, tough to move on that way. That's why I'm still here in Moab, and hangin' with Brendan and Sammy. I realized a few years ago that I needed to move on from where I was at that time—or die."

I laughed at where I was, who I was with, and what he was talking about. My body was adjusting to the hot water and I began to relax. "Is that what Brendan asked you to talk to me about? Moving on?"

"Ah, no, man. I just got sidetracked. I'm supposed to be talkin' to you about support."

"I thought you said you didn't do support groups."

"I don't. But I know I wouldn't be here without a lot of support. And I don't think you would be either."

I thought for a moment. "I guess you're right, Preacher. I *am* off track—using your words, I'm screwed up. Sometimes the 'f' word is the only one that cuts to the chase. And you're right about me having support. I have a great family, good friends and people who have put up with a lot from me."

"They supporting you now? I don't see any of them here. Were they helping you move on?"

Man, another question-asker. Why am I not surprised. "You know, you ask a lot of questions. You really a preacher?"

I thought he smiled, but wasn't sure. "No, not formally. I was never dunked in no river or anything like that. I just like to talk a lot and people seem to listen, so one night an old friend of mine—poor guy's dead now—called me preacher in a bar. I think it was in Cave Creek, Arizona. Some good bars there, great country music and square dancing. Anyhow, it got a good laugh from the folks around, and it just stuck. But I'm not going to let you sidetrack me again. I could never look Brendan in the eyes if I didn't do what I promised to do. So let me ask you again. Are any of your people supporting you now?"

An image of Preacher square dancing crossed my mind. As is often the case, I figured he was probably the last guy I'd imagine as a good dancer, but he was probably great. "Well I guess so. My mom says my sister and brothers call a lot to ask how I am, my friends, too."

"Before you came out here—from Philly, right?"

I nodded.

"How were you gettin' their support back there?"

I slid down farther so that my shoulders were fully submerged in the steaming water and out of the cool desert air.

"I don't know. I had a few beers with my buddies one night, and my mom and I talked quite a bit."

"So did you really try to get some support from them? Or did you just kind of hang out with them when they showed up? Huge difference you know."

I shrugged. Not sure how to answer this one.

"What I mean is this, man. It's impossible to do it alone. You hear me? And by it I mean the life we are all trying to make for ourselves. This stuff that Brendan talks about looks simple, but its deep, really deep, man. I really buy into that whole creating a vision thing…and I know that there ain't none of us who can turn a vision into reality without asking for help. Those things feed off one another, kind of build on one another."

"I think I get that we all need some help… but I'm not sure what you mean by saying they feed off each other."

Preacher swiveled his head to look at me. "They enhance one another. Like that word, 'enhance'? Just started using that one, I heard Brendan use it. None of us know everything we need to know to make our visions a reality. If we knew everything, we'd be God. So we've got to look around for people who are smarter than us… and in my case that ain't hard."

I wouldn't swear to it, but I think Preacher winked at me before he continued speaking. "And once we start talking with other people, and getting their help and encouragement, our vision changes. It starts to turn into the reality we want. It's that simple."

"I think I get it," I said. "I'm not sure that I have a vision yet, but I do know that what I imagine for my future changes every time I talk to somebody out here."

"You got it," said Preacher. "And that's one of the things I like about Brendan's Jackrabbit thing. All the principles are connected to one another. It's why it works for so many people, me included."

"Yeah, I'm starting to see that. Actually, I'm starting to kind of feel them."

"Good." Preacher raised his ink-covered arms to the sky and locked his fingers as he lowered them to rest on the back of his head. "And I hope you do for a long, long time."

"Have you done this... asked for help, for support?"

"Not always, but nearly every day now, man, sometimes I ask for help from my friends and family, people like Brendan, and Paul and Sammy. That's what Brendan calls 'external' support—looking outside of yourself. Know what I mean?"

I nodded.

"Then other times I just take time to be still, as Vanessa would say. I do the internal work—that's Brendan's word, too—all the thinking that we have to do for ourselves. Some forms of support are real powerful, others not so much. It depends."

"I'm not sure I get this external versus internal thing," I said. "What does that really mean?" I took in a deep breath, not sure where this lesson was going.

Preacher watched a small green bird flutter into a desert bush. "Well, the external ones are just that, they're outside of us. They're the people and all the stuff that can help get you focused—or refocused—when you need it. They can make you laugh or cry when you need that, or make you see things differently when maybe that's what you need. I remember once when I was feeling bad because I'd just been fired from a job and didn't have no money. I ran into Benny at the Center. You know Benny, right? The rich dude. Well, I didn't feel like talkin' to anyone that rich at the time, but he saw that I was down and got me talking. Then he told me that he'd been fired nine times in his career! Get that, man! Nine times! That's way more than I've been fired. Anyway, as corny as it may sound, Benny said that because of all the practice he'd had at being fired, he'd gotten really good at coping with it, and getting past it. And he learned to use it as opportunity to try doing something really different with his life. And that gave me a new way to think about my own situation. Get it?"

I nodded.

"Sometimes, we just need to look away from something that's going on in our life, because chances are we'll see it differently when we look back at it."

"So this support you're talking about... sounds like you didn't think much of me getting support from my family and friends."

"The people in your life are a main source of support, but it's a real powerful two-way street, man. You gotta keep an eye out for the kind of energy they are giving you. And that you're giving them. Do you really know which people in your life are your best support network? The ones that love you no matter what? The ones who want you to succeed and be well? The ones you could call anytime—day or night—and ask for anything, and they'd deliver?"

"I guess so. I mean I never really thought about it, but I think I do." I lifted some water in my cupped hands then let it drip through my fingers as the faces of my mom and dad, my sisters and brothers, and good friends raced across my mind.

"You need to know who they are, man, especially with where you're at. I once heard a doctor buddy of mine tell the story about when his dad passed away. He and I played linebacker together way back in college. Well, he played a few more years than I did." Preacher shook his head and grinned mischievously at me. "The folks in charge asked if I'd consider leaving the squad. Actually they didn't ask. I see this guy from time to time; he's been good to me. His dad had been sick and getting worse for almost a year. At the end he was in the hospital and really near death. He said the whole family had come to see him, except for his son-in-law and granddaughter, who were driving in from a few states away. Anyhow, shortly after they arrived and said their good-byes, the man died. My friend said it was as if his dad knew they weren't there yet, even when he was so out of it. Some part of him knew he had to let them say goodbye to him.

"My buddy said this—and I'll never forget it—he said that his dad's vital signs were *incompatible with life*. Now, there's a million dollar phrase for you. *Incompatible with life*. What it means to me is that this guy's will to be with some of his support network—his spirit—was stronger than the worldly facts of medicine and biology. To me, that says something... maybe it says everything."

Preacher scratched at his beard. "Do your people know that they play this role in your life? Have you told them how much they mean to you? And how grateful you are to have them in your life? And how much you need them?"

I watched the bird fly from the bush. "I don't know. Good questions."

"Jake, it's like this. I read a story one time about a town near the ocean that had lots of canneries—and because of this they also had a bunch of pelicans all over the place. And reading, by the way, is a great way of getting external support. I plan on doing more of it, but I don't read too fast so it takes me a long time."

"Anyway, the canneries would process the fish and seafood and then toss the scraps back into the ocean, or into garbage cans. All the fish parts and waste would be served up every day for the pelicans to eat. I guess it would be like us going to a free smorgasbord every day. They were the guests of the town."

I sank under the water for a moment and then surfaced. "Preacher, can I ask a question?"

"Sure."

"Where in the heck are you going with this?"

Preacher's laugh echoed off the canyon walls. "After many years the town began to slip. Tourists stopped coming as newer beach towns popped up. The fishing got worse, and because of this, many of the canneries closed."

"Not good?"

"Nope. Not good for anyone, especially the pelicans. You see, they'd gotten real spoiled, and it was so easy for them that they forgot how to get food for themselves. And the town had a problem because these birds were what a cop friend of mine would call a public nuisance. They were attacking little kids with French fries, and raiding people's trash and restaurant dumpsters. It wasn't a good situation."

"So what'd the town do?"

"Well, a couple people wanted to kill the birds. Some wanted to ignore the problem, thinking it would go away on its own. Never does though. Then one guy—a pretty wise dude— came to one of the city council meetings and asked, 'Why don't we get some wild pelicans and bring 'em here?' Most folks said that would just make things worse, more birds seeking food. The man agreed. But then he made his point. He said that the wild birds are still used to getting food by hunting in the ocean and bays. He figured the wild pelicans would help the lazy ones learn to take care of themselves again.'"

I hung on Preacher's words. When he finally took a breath, I jumped at the chance to ask a question. "Did it work?"

"Did it work? Did it work? Of course it worked, my man. Jake, do you really think I'd tell you a story to make a point that didn't make the point? What in the world are you people doing in Philly?" He splashed water at my face.

Laughing I raised my hands to shield myself. "Okay, okay."

"It worked because of a basic principle of human nature, and I guess maybe pelican nature too. The lazy pelicans became like the ones they began to hang out with, the ones that would go and work for their food. Just like us, you become very much like the people you hang with, you become like your support network. I don't mean the same people, but I mean the same values, the same principles, the same work ethic, the same way of knowing right from wrong, and the same ability—or lack of—to develop vision and create reality. Ridin' with some of the guys I used to hang with, I was one twisted dude—just like them. Get it?"

I was thinking of some of the people I'd hung around over the past few years, some good, some maybe not so good.

"So what do you think?" Preacher sat back as his arms floated in front of him, moving slowly back and forth.

"It makes sense. Maybe the people I used to hang with weren't exactly twisted dudes, but some I wouldn't take home to meet my parents. And recently… since the accident… I haven't really been letting many people into my world at all, especially those in my support network."

"Well, Jake," Preacher took a gulp of water, and then spit it over the side of the steel tub, "you might want to start now. Seems to me like there's a lot of people, perhaps we can call them your pelican posse…" He chuckled. "That are fixin' to help you get right again. You want to get back on the right track? Start hanging out with people that are on their own right tracks. And not just others, but you, too, hang out with yourself.

"It's simple," he continued. "You want to be happy—hang with happy people. You want to be positive—hang with positive people. You want to be successful—hang with successful people."

I thought of all the calls and visits I'd gotten from my friends, especially my friend Joe, my sister, and Lauren. I was definitely shutting them out.

"How do you know so much about this? From hangin' out with bikers?"

"Nope...Jail." Preacher laughed. "I had been there a half dozen times or so, sometimes overnight. Other times for a lot longer." He paused, and then continued, "Heck, Jake, I used to hang with some of the most stupid, drugged out, ignorant asses on the planet. And do you know what I got?"

"What?"

"I got to exist for about fifteen years as a world-class stupid, drugged out, ignorant ass myself. And it's not just because I hung with bikers. Bikers get a bad rap. Man, there's so many wonderful, caring, hard-working bikers out there it ain't even funny. But some of 'em — " He shook his head. "It doesn't matter what you do, or what you have. You don't think there aren't a bunch of these people—some on drugs and some not—all over? Sammy said Wall Street's full of 'em. A friend of mine's a big-shot in software sales and he said there are plenty of them in that industry, too."

Preacher paused for a moment. "But it ain't about them. It's about you and the people in your life, and the people that want to be in your life. C'mon, man, you gotta let those people in."

"Yeah. I think I need to. But Preacher, you said a minute ago that it was not just them, but me too. You said for me to hang out with myself. What'd you mean?"

He turned his head toward a noise, and Canyon appeared, coming up the path. The dog climbed to the high side of the hill, took a seat and looked at us. Preacher moved to the side of the tub, reaching over to rub Canyon's head as he continued.

"There's the external side of your support network, but there's another side—perhaps even more powerful—the internal. Take reading. Thoreau, you know that guy who went out and lived in the woods for a few years, asked, 'How many men have penned a new chapter of their lives from the reading of a book?' Right now, close your eyes and come up with ways that you can support yourself. I'll give you a minute."

I closed my eyes. The voice inside my head began. How do I support myself? I don't know. What's he talking about? I understand what he's saying so far, about others, and books, but how can I support me? I opened my eyes.

"Preacher, I need some help here. I'm not coming up with anything."

"It's okay, dude. One of my favorite examples is Abraham Lincoln. Paul told me—he's a real Lincoln fan, you know—anyway, he told me Old Abe had a pretty tough life. He came from a poor background, lost a couple of businesses, and had to deal with the deaths of two sons. He lost a lot of elections, and then when he did become President—one of the finest of all times—he had to deal with slavery and the Civil War. Pretty heavy stuff. But Abe's a great example of a person seeking internal support. Paul told me a quote from Abe that went like this, 'I have been driven to my knees many times by the overwhelming conviction that I have nowhere else to go.' You see, Jake, Abe went inside, found the time to be still, and prayed. That's the connection between stillness and internal support. This probably worked well for Abe because of his deep sense of what he often referred to as the Divine."

"You know, Preacher, for a guy who doesn't read a lot, you sure have some good quotes."

"Truth be told, I'm not a great reader. But I do read some, I have a great memory, and I listen very closely when Paul and Brendan talk. I like quotes and I try real hard to remember 'em."

"I know what you mean about Lincoln. I used to pray a lot, but then stopped when… well, anyway, now I want to make it habit… though I have to admit I'm out of practice. I do believe in

God. I know He's real, and that this life's not all there is. There's more after our bodies stop working."

"And how's that praying working out for you?" said Preacher.

"This morning's session was pretty good. I could really feel myself slowing down… being still."

"Well then, you may want to keep doing it. Life—to me— is just a big experiment. You become aware of something that ain't right for you, find another way of thinking about it, and then just experiment and try some new things for a while. You know, Jake, I've tried talkin' to some of my old buddies about Jackrabbit and they try to make fun of me. They say I'm getting caught up in a dumb theory, and start callin' me Philosopher instead of Preacher. I say there's nothing wrong with having a philosophy—and really, it's a great thing, especially if it leads to action. And that's what Jackrabbit has done for me. I remember when Sammy and I were having a beer once and we had a great conversation about Brendan and Jackrabbit. She told me that a theory is a 'proposed explanation for something.' So, Jackrabbit—for me—is the explanation why some people are happy and fulfilled most of the time, and others aren't."

"I realize that now." I sank back into the water, letting out my breath and letting water run through my hair. "At first I thought you were all a bunch of old hippies or granola eaters." I glanced at Preacher, and realized maybe I'd made a mistake. "And if you are… well, that's OK. But I see now that what you are all practicing out there… this way of thinking, these prin-ciples for engaging with life, are very connected to action. I love the fact that the two-sided arrow at the center of the Jackrabbit philosophy represents action. This has really helped me start to change my thinking. I remember a quote, you may like this one.

It goes something like, 'I do not know if action brings happiness, but I know that there is no happiness without action.'"

Preacher gave Canyon a pat on the head and leaned his head back, a drop of water hanging from his hoop earring. "Yeah, man, I love it. And I'd add that the action needs to be pointed at a clear vision. And another thing, my man, Jake, there's tremendous power in what we say to ourselves. The things we say to ourselves all the time, that's probably our best kind of support. You can't really control what others say to you, or about you. But you can absolutely control what you say to yourself. It ain't always easy to do, but it sure is doable.

"I think of it like having a radio in my head. And I get to choose the channel. So do me—no do *yourself*—a favor and really begin to tune in to your internal chatter. What you put in is really connected to what comes out. If you're talking yourself down, change the channel. As soon as you wake up every morning, say something good to yourself. Even when you have a tough day ahead, or life's really beating the piss out of you, just begin the day with some good input. Trust me, man, it's magic."

I looked at Preacher as he closed his eyes and leaned his head back again. I was thinking that our lesson was over. "So, that's it? Focus on my external support network, as well as my internal chatter and let others, and myself, help me?"

He opened one eye, his head still resting on the tub. "Not totally, one more thing. There's also a connection to your happiness and fulfillment that comes not just from getting support, but by also giving it."

Preacher lifted his head. "I have to get going, and you probably do too. So a quick story that should help you get it. I once had a great job of working with an organization that grants wishes to sick kids. It was during a time when I was hangin' with some generous, volunteering bikers. Go figure, right? Anyhow, during that time, I worked on a wish for a teenager who had cancer in his leg, he'd actually had to have the lower part of his leg amputated within a year after I met him. He never complained, never felt sorry for himself. So we work with this great young dude and get him a shopping spree for the day, with a limo to take him around. He got a certain amount of money for each year of his age, and he was thirteen. Plus me and my wish partner got him some extra gift certificates from some cool people at this mall. Long story short, he has about $2,400 to spend. Imagine a teenager with the green light to spend over two grand."

I nodded.

"Well, it took him a little time to get going. He bought some things for his brother, and his little sister. All he really wanted was a basketball hoop. He loved hoops and was really good, even with his bum leg. He used to beat me a lot when we'd play horse. Anyhow, we're looking at hoops and I'm telling him to go for this kick-butt, really nice hoop and he's just like, 'I don't know.' I mean this thing was fiberglass and adjustable, it was exactly what he'd told me many times he wanted. So I tell him to chill out and keep looking and I take a walk with his mom. They were a family going through some hard times financially, and in other ways. His mom tells me that morning she talked to him and told him she really wanted him to have a good time and spend the money. She then told me that he—this young 13-year old kid with cancer—looked right into her eyes and said, 'But mom, this is a lot of money, I just want to make sure you're alright.'" Preacher stopped, looking off into the distance.

He turned back to me. "Get it?"

I nodded strongly, and then reached over to shake Preacher's hand.

We sat quietly for a moment in the tub, both caught in the power of Preacher's story. I asked the name of this principle and he told me.

He climbed out of the tub with just a wink and a smile, and as he began walking down the path with Canyon at his side, I chuckled at what was written across the butt of his of black Speedo: Property of Hell's Angels.

I leaned my head back on the edge of the tub, the first rays of sun warming my face. I began to breathe very slowly and deeply.

Sometime later, I returned to the bunkhouse and sat down at the table. With marker and now well-worn Jackrabbit diagram in front of me, I captured the final Jackrabbit principle that Preacher had so simply and powerfully explained to me: SEEK SUPPORT.

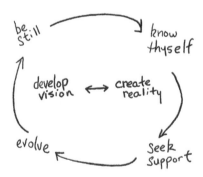

Later that night I called Lauren. I hadn't talked to her since before I left Pennsylvania.

"Hello."

I liked the sound of her voice, and part of me wished I was right there with her. "Hi Lauren, it's me."

"Oh hey. How are you? I've been thinking about you. Really—how are you?"

"Well, I think I'm doing much better. I've met some really cool people and I feel like…" I stopped at the sound of a man's voice in the background. The voice called out, "Who is it? We have to leave in a few minutes."

"Who's that?" My voice was sharper than I meant it to be.

"Oh, it's just a friend. We're going to meet some people, so I've got to get going."

My heart sank and for the second time in my life I felt an overpowering jolt course through my body. And though this time it was less physical, the pain was just as real. *Crap, I knew she'd find somebody; I bet it's one of the guys from the beach. Probably John, that guy who's always nice to me and thinks I don't know he likes Lauren. He was probably happy to hear about my accident. Why didn't I let her help? Why have I been shutting her out?*

"Jake?" Her voice stopped my chatter. "You still there?"

I couldn't think of what to say. I called to apologize for not letting her in after the accident, but I was so surprised that the words had deserted me. *Why do I feel so bad about her having a date? How stupid is this to be surprised that Lauren is having fun after the way I treated her?* I fought the urge to hang up, or to sarcastically tell her I was okay and to have a good time with whomever she was with tonight. She deserved better than that, especially from me.

I cleared my throat. "Lauren, I know you've got to go but just listen to me for a minute. Number one, I hope you have a great time tonight with whoever's there, whether he's just a friend, or maybe even something more. And I mean that. Number two, I just want to say I'm sorry for not letting you help me after the accident. I know now that you were trying to support me in whatever way I needed, and I didn't let you. And I'm real sorry for that. That's all."

She was quiet for a moment. "Thanks, Jake. Can we talk later? Maybe in a day or two?"

"Sure, Lauren. I'd like that. Goodnight… and take care."

"You too, Jake. Goodnight."

I waited for her to hang up first, secretly wishing she'd say something else to me. But what? Just something, anything. She didn't. I sat there a long time. I knew I'd done the right thing, treating Lauren as she deserved rather than how my ego wanted to handle it. But here again was a reminder that I couldn't simply wish away the past few months.

22

Moving On

"I find that in this world it is not so much where we stand, as in what direction we are moving."

–Oliver Wendell Holmes

I slept fitfully that night, waking off and on to check the clock and search my mind for a face to match the voice I heard in the background during my call to Lauren. I finally dragged myself out of bed a little after 6:30 and pulled on my running shoes. But then I reminded myself of my resolve to start each day with stillness. *Please, God, help me out here. I feel like I'm moving in the right direction, then I talk with Lauren and I feel like I'm still stuck. I get that You can't—or better yet—You choose not to control all the happenings here on Earth, but sometimes it sure would be easier for us if You did.*

A few birds flitted in and out among some boulders on the hillside as I stared out the window. *I guess I'm just asking You to hang around, or give me a little kick to get me officially unstuck.* I laughed at my use of the word "officially," but I figured God would know what that means.

I rose and took a run through the silent desert, the first rays of sunlight illuminating the distant clouds. I returned to the house, a bit more energized, pulled off my shoes and socks, and settled into the lone chair in the bunkhouse. Then a growl rolled up from my stomach, a signal to slip on my sandals and head out the front door. Approaching the main house I saw Paul sitting on the front porch, his navy bag at his side.

"You off somewhere?"

He smiled as he saw me. "Oh, good morning, Jake. Yep, I'm heading back home, just waiting on Sammy to pick me up and drive me to the airport. I figured I'd see you before I left. How are you?"

"Feeling okay. I think I'm going to head out myself in a few days, after Brendan gets back. Seems like time to get home and get this figured out."

"Great, but be sure to talk with Brendan so you've got that clear vision for when you leave. You should know the importance of that."

"I am, and I'm trying to be more aware every day."

"So, I'm leaving in a little while and I wanted to chat with you one more time. Let's sit. "He motioned to the chair next to him.

I nodded, noticing Paul's thin arms and neck, and the gray pallor of his skin. He'd seemed pretty strong during our bike ride the day before, but right now, he looked a decade older.

"You remember we were talking about 'evolve' yesterday?"

I nodded.

"Well, there's one more thing I want you to consider. I know you'll begin to work with the principles of Jackrabbit, I mean really live them. You've lived some of them before, probably without even knowing it. But I believe you'll now strive to live them more completely, consistently, more intensely, but in a relaxed way—a natural way."

I looked at my sandals, then back to Paul. "Yep, I think I will." *Will I really? Or am I just saying this?*

"Oh, you will. And it's my hope—and part of my vision for you—that you'll offer these to others."

I stood as I saw Sammy's Jeep coming up the road. "You know I've always kind of thought about talking to groups of people."

Paul stood up to join me. "And you will—quite successfully, I imagine. Listen, Jake, some people will be very open and receptive to this message. Many want it. They need it. But one thing I know for sure is that many people view our way of thinking, our way of engaging with this life and our world as fluff, as hippy stuff, as only for people from California."

I laughed.

Paul rolled his eyes. "Quite simply, they think this is B.S., that it's not important, it doesn't contribute to their life. Do me one favor, Jake, will you?" Paul paused, his eyes staring deep into mine.

"Sure, what?"

He stepped close, his arms wrapping around my shoulders, and I felt his breath against my ear.

"Help them reconsider."

A chill spread across my back and down my arms as we parted.

I spun toward the rising sun and thought about—no, saw—in that instant I saw myself in a large auditorium with a microphone on the lapel of my shirt, wearing jeans and sandals and a white dress shirt with the sleeves rolled up. I was talking to a large crowd, and they were listening. I was talking about Jackrabbit and how it had helped me and how it could help others. *This is what vision is all about. That was how my love of philosophy and helping and everything else could become reality.*

Sammy pulled a U-turn in the open area between us and the bunkhouse and stopped right in front of us. She jumped out and came around to give Paul a hug as I tossed Paul's bag into the back seat. She turned to hug me, and asked if I could help out with some painting at the bar that morning. I quickly agreed, glad there was nothing weird in her attitude toward me after my failed romantic gesture back in the desert.

Just before they began to pull away I leaned into the window and put my hand on Paul's bony shoulder. "I'll stop to see you on the way home in the next week or so. Sound good?"

"Sounds great. Be well, Jake." A peaceful smile spread on his face as he turned and gazed through the windshield.

Sammy gave me a little wave as they pulled away. They disappeared into a plume of dust as I walked into the main house. I made some coffee then decided to explore the house a little. Steaming mug of coffee in hand, I scanned the many books stacked on tables and shelves. Walking into Brendan's office one got my attention; it was a small brown hardback nestled at the end of a row of various sized books against a silver lion bookend. I opened the inside cover and saw a note, handwritten in faded blue ink.

B – Thanks for your guidance, you are truly a gift to many people, myself included! Enjoy the book.

I came across the quote below and thought of you
and our coaching work.
"Renew thyself completely each day,
do it again, and again, and forever again."
Beautiful, yes? It's supposedly a Chinese inscrip-
tion cited by Thoreau in Walden. Anyhow, thanks
again. Look forward to connecting in the future.

Be well.

Bobby

I stayed in the office for a while, then drank the last swig of my coffee, cleaned the mug, placing it back into the simple wooden cabinet. *Hmm, wonder who Bobby is.* I jumped into my pickup and drove off to Sammy's to help paint a section of the kitchen.

The sky was clear and the air warmed as I pulled around the back of the restaurant and walked in the kitchen door. Sammy stood with Mike, the guy I'd seen when I was sitting in the parking lot on my first day in Moab. He was the one who walked out back and stood for a moment with his face turned toward the sun. I'd been in his company a few times. He was a Texan, about fifty, who'd grown up on a ranch and was on the professional rodeo circuit in his younger years.

"Hey, Sammy. Hi, Mike."

Sammy wore khaki hiking shorts with large pockets on the side and a navy blue t-shirt with a gold logo right in the middle on the front.

"Oh, hey Jake. Thanks for coming. Mike and you should be able to knock out the painting in a few hours. It's not too bad, just needs a fresh coat."

"We'll need to." Mike winked at me. "So I can be ready to work lunch."

"We'll be fine." She patted Mike's back. "Just let me go grab the paint." As she turned and walked out of the room I noticed the two words on the back of her t-shirt: be still.

"Hey, Sammy, what's with the t-shirt?"

She smiled back over her shoulder, "You like it? Well, you treat me nice and I'll see what I can do about getting you one."

"And what's the logo on the front?"

Mike took his hat off and showed the same logo to me. "Look familiar?"

I studied it. "Kind of looks like a rabbit."

"Man." Mike laughed in Sammy's direction. "He really is bright. Yes, Jake, it's a rabbit, but not just any rabbit. This would be a jackrabbit."

"Oh, yeah, I see it." The logo was designed with the simplicity of a Picasso sketch.

Sammy was pulling paint brushes from a box. "I had an idea for a clothing line. Something fun, that could help people stay aware of Jackrabbit—if they found it to be of value in their lives. The best way to create change is to stay conscious of the change you want, and continue to watch your behavior. Pretty hard to ignore something when you're wearing it, right? At this point we only have t-shirts and caps, but I can see it getting bigger—people are loving it. The best thing is that a good portion of the profits go to great causes, and some of it stays right here at the Tuscany Wellness Center."

"Give me a half dozen of each. I can think of quite a few folks at home—my support network—that would love these."

She gave me thumbs up. "We can make that happen. I've got to leave now to run some errands. See you guys later."

Mike and I began to paint, but at first the color appeared lighter than expected. "It'll darken as it dries," I said. Mike nodded, then turned on the CD player and started singing along with the music. I felt like I was at a benefit concert as songs by Clapton, the Beatles, Springsteen and Tom Petty filled the kitchen. There were also a few from a new singer I liked, Tim Severance. Mike told me that in the past three years Severance had released two albums, had four number one songs, and won three Grammy's. Listening to his music, I could understand his popularity.

A few hours later the door swung open and Sammy popped her head in as I was washing out the brushes in the back sink. "Hey, thanks a lot for your help. The painting looks great. When you finish up here come into the restaurant and I'll buy you lunch for helping me out. I have someone I want you to meet."

I put the paint supplies and leftover paint down in the basement and walked through the kitchen into the restaurant. Sammy was sitting at the end of the bar with a man. She waved me over. The guy wore an army green v-neck t-shirt and jeans.

Sammy stood and grabbed my hand.

"Jake, this is my friend Tim. Tim, Jake."

We shook hands. Tim had short brown hair, blue eyes, and a relaxed manner. Then it struck me just who I had shaken hands with. "You're Tim Severance, right? This is crazy. Mike and I just listened to some of your music in the kitchen. And I must confess, he does a pretty good impersonation of you — should you ever be looking for a backup."

"I'll keep that in mind."

We all laughed and Sammy pulled me toward the barstool. "Come on, Jake, sit down. Let's get some lunch." Tori, the bartender, came over and took our orders. I thought of grabbing a Guinness, but instead got a glass of water.

Over lunch, the three of us chatted about the weather, a few kids at Tuscany, the bike race coming to town, and the pending pro football season, at which point Sammy stood. "I've got to run out and do some more errands, so you two have a great time finishing your lunch." She put her hand on Tim's shoulder. "I'll catch up with you later, Tori." She waved, "no bill for these two today; lunch is on me. But make sure they tip the bartender." Sammy leaned in and kissed Tim on the cheek and then me.

Tim told me he was originally from upstate New York, near Lake Placid, and had moved to LA a few years after college. One thing he said really struck me. "I had a few full-time jobs after college and I fooled with my music, but I didn't see a fulfilling future in what I was doing. I just kept thinking—over and over—that what I really wanted to focus on was making music. That thought got so strong and became such a companion of mine, that I got to a point where I had no choice. And as often happens, many of my family and friends said I was crazy, that it was such a tough business." He was staring at his glass, wiping moisture from the side. "You know, all that kind of stuff."

I was amazed at how Tim was so down-to-earth. During lunch two young girls had approached and asked for his autograph and he was very gracious, posing for a picture with them and finding out where they were from.

A man in a crimson sweatshirt with a big H on the front waved at Tim as he walked toward the front door. "How'd you ever find this place?" I asked him.

He turned to me, sliding his plate away. "Well, Sammy and I went to college together and have been friends since then. We met at a restaurant on campus where we worked. After she left New York and moved here she invited me for a visit. I finally made it out—and as you've probably experienced—I fell in love with the place. That was about five years ago. It's funny... since I've been coming here I have had much more success with my career." He took a sip of water. "Maybe funny is the wrong word."

"So you think coming here has helped your career?"

"Well…" He took a deep breath. "Probably not the actual act of coming here, but more so what I do when I'm here, and how I've really learned to think differently and be different since meeting Brendan and talking more with Sammy and Bennie."

Mike walked from the kitchen, drying his hands and gave us a nod. "You know the whole crowd here? Bennie and Vanessa and Paul, as well?" I asked.

"Absolutely, know 'em all, and consider them friends. We were actually able to bring five kids from Tuscany to my concert in Denver on Bennie's jet last year. Man was that great. I'm really thankful…" he placed his hands together like I saw folks do at the end of their yoga session "…to have them in my life. Great people."

"So you said you learned to think differently. What do you mean? Jackrabbit?"

Tim nodded and smiled as Tori came and cleared our plates.

"Do you think Jackrabbit works for anybody, even famous people like you?"

He shifted on the stool, shaking his head a bit, and running his hand through his hair. "Thanks, Jake, I know you mean that as a compliment, but I don't consider myself any different or more important from anyone else just because of what I do. We all have jobs and careers, it just seems like more people know me. And that's really good for me and my career, but I don't think it really separates me from other folks. And remember, when I consciously began—I guess I was doing a little of this thinking— but when I really got focused on applying the Jackrabbit principles I was just another of the thousands of unknown musicians living in LA. Yep, I think it can work for anybody, so long as they work it, and take some action, and so long as they're open to change. A friend of Brendan's, an old drummer I met here a few years ago, told me that for him Jackrabbit is just a mindset, a framework for thinking."

I nodded. "So how often do you come out?"

"Well, my schedule is pretty crazy as it is, so not as often as I'd like. I guess two or three times a year for a few days. I'm thinking of coming out for about a month next year to write some songs for my next album. I try to keep my head pretty clear and relaxed as much as I can, but there are always tons of distractions coming at me in LA and on the road when I'm touring. It's really cool to come out here and be still with more intensity. When my mind relaxes I'm much more creative. I write more songs, and I think they're purer, more authentic for me."

"So what's your favorite principle of Jackrabbit?" I asked, feeling a little like a talk show host.

"Ah, man that's a tough one—I love 'em all. But okay, let me think for a moment. Which is my favorite?" Tim turned on the barstool to gaze out the window. "Yep." He said as he turned back. "My favorite is develop vision and create reality. There's so much power and inspiration for me when I set my mind to developing a vision for something that's nowhere other than in my mind, just sitting and imagining a part or time of my life that hasn't happened yet. Then I'll usually write out that vision. That's what I did when I left here after my first visit, I saw myself signing a record deal. Then after that happened, I saw myself receiving a Grammy, I even wrote my acceptance speech. How's that for vision?"

His lips closed and eyes narrowed. His voice was soft as he continued. "And then it came true. That was very cool when my name was called and I went to the stage and gave that brief speech, the same one I'd written years before it happened. I was thanking folks and sharing some quick thoughts, but I'd done it before many, many times. I'd say it when stopped at traffic lights, sometimes when out for a run. You see, that moment I was having had happened in my mind a whole bunch of times. But the key—for me—is the double-sided arrow at the middle of the diagram, action. I've come to strongly believe that not much happens without action."

I laughed. "Yeah, I'll bet that was pretty wild."

"So how about you? Sammy told me a little about your accident. She didn't think you'd mind because she knew we'd talk. Is that cool?"

"Yeah, that's fine." *Wonder how much she told him. Did she tell him about me trying to kiss her afterward? Wonder if these two are more than friends.* "Well, I'm trying to figure out what to do. I think I have a good idea, but sometimes I still..." I struggled for a moment to describe how I felt. "I still feel a bit, in the words of my friend Preacher, a bit screwed up."

Tim burst out laughing. All the patrons in the bar turned our way for a moment. "Oh man, that Preacher—I love that guy. He asked if he could tour with me as my bodyguard. I said sure, but he said he was only messing with me. He didn't need that lifestyle again. So how'd you meet Preacher? Here at Sammy's?"

I took a sip of water, letting out a quick laugh as I recalled my first visit to Sammy's and my fear of the guy at the end of the bar with all the tattoos. "No...well I guess, yes. I saw him here the first day I got to Moab, and he scared the crap out of me. We met for real just yesterday morning, in the hot tub at Brendan's place. He talked to me about seeking support."

"Yeah, me too. Although not in a hot tub. I can only imagine that scene. Preacher and I took a ride on a couple of his bikes. He let me ride a vintage Harley. We stopped to grab some gas and a soda and as we sat on a bench out front of the gas station, he talked to me about the importance of seeking—and providing—support. I remember it well."

"Did he tell you the about the pelicans?"

"Oh, yeah." Tim nodded. "It was a cool story—really made a strong point for me. When I went back to LA I took a good look at who I was hanging with and decided I needed to change my pelican posse. Some people stayed, others went, and other new folks began to show up. I also started to offer support to others. One of the things I look forward to—and never did before—is to volunteer at a shelter for the homeless in LA. For me, there's something powerfully present when I help others."

I nodded as Tim placed a $20 bill on the bar for Tori. I reached into my pocket and he stopped me. "Jake, I got it, it's been great to meet you and talk some. I've gotta run now. I want to visit a few folks, and then I'm out of here early tomorrow. Here's my number in case you ever just want to talk—about anything. Let me know if you get to LA, and I'll let you know when we're going to be in Philly. Give me your number. I'd love for you and some family or friends to come to a show." I wrote my number on a bar napkin and gave it to Tim, then we hugged goodbye. I seemed to be getting good at this hugging thing.

"Thanks, Tim, great timing for our talk as I'm probably getting out of here soon." He turned toward the door with a smile and nod. I watched as he held the door for an older couple that had no idea who he was.

23

The End of the Beginning

"The most important thing about moving on, is to know when to move on."

–Danny Bader

A few days later, I sat in the kitchen of Brendan's house rubbing Canyon's head. A steaming mug of coffee sat before me on the simple wood table. I'd risen early, performed my "be still" ritual of prayer, and then taken Canyon on a hike while the sky was still full of orange, blue and purple.

I pulled the well-worn Jackrabbit paper from my back pocket and unfolded it on the table. I'd been trying for the past few days to focus on developing my vision more, starting from that tantalizing image of myself teaching Jackrabbit that I'd had after talking with Paul, but nothing was clear yet. I thought about the things I'd loved doing all my life—thinking about the meaning of life, studying philosophy, helping people, being true to my faith. Could helping people understand Jackrabbit allow me to bring it all together into a life, I wondered.

I sipped my coffee, hearing only Canyon's breathing, and jumped at the ring of the old black phone hanging on the wall. I picked it up on the second one.

"Hello."

"Hey, Jake, it's Brendan."

"Oh, hey, Brendan. How are you? I think Canyon's missing you. He's been hanging out with me, but I can tell he wants to walk with you in the morning, not me. He keeps looking back at the house the whole time. What's up?"

"Well, Jake, you know I was going to be home at the beginning of next week, but there's been a change in plans. I'll be home tomorrow. I've got to get some clothes I didn't bring on the trip. I'm only coming home for a day and then heading back out. I was hoping you'll join me."

"Where?"

Brendan didn't respond right away. "We have to go to Columbus, Jake. Paul died."

My chin dropped to my chest as I sank to the floor against the kitchen cabinets. We were both quiet. Tears filled my eyes, and I suddenly needed some water.

"Jake?"

"Yeah. Yeah, I'm here. What happened? How'd you find out?"

"Well, Mo called me this morning. Seems Paul hadn't really gotten out of bed but a few times after he got home earlier this week. She said he was really tired before the trip out here, so I'm guessing he really wanted to be up and in a good mood when he came to see us. He must have known. The family was with him last night as he went to sleep. Mo said he still had his sense of humor despite his very low energy. She sat with him for a few hours after he fell asleep. She didn't know why she stayed, but she did. She kissed him on his forehead around midnight and then went to bed. This morning when she went in, he had passed."

"Man, this sucks." I wiped my nose on my sleeve and glanced at Canyon, who was now lying on his side, looking up at me.

"Yes. Yes, it does. So you'll come with me?"

"Yeah, absolutely. I guess I'll just drive from here to Columbus, then head on home."

"Sounds good." Brendan paused. "And Jake."

"Yeah?"

"This is going to hurt today and for some time. Have a good day with your thoughts, think about Paul, pray if you feel like it, but stay moving forward. I'll see you tomorrow."

"Yeah, okay. I mean I'll try. Thanks for calling, Brendan."

I spent the rest of the day walking, praying and thinking, mostly praying. I did have some beers, but only two. I sure wanted to have more, but I didn't. I packed much of my stuff and called my mom. She said she was sad to hear about Paul, and that she knew how much I liked him and how it seemed that he had helped me get better. She ended telling me she loved me and was happy I was coming home.

After Brendan arrived we planned our trip, deciding to set out before sunrise the next morning. Brendan would drive with me to Columbus and then fly back to Moab with Benny. We'd drive most of the first day, stopping sometime after dinner to sleep. This way we figured we'd complete the sixteen-hundred-mile journey early in the evening on our second day of travel. Brendan asked me to call John—the groundskeeper for Tuscany—to arrange for him to look after Canyon.

We went to Tuscany later in the day so I could say goodbye to some of the folks I'd met, especially Noah. I searched and finally found him sleeping. He'd been receiving some different treatments, and they made him very tired. I stood for a moment at his bedside, watching his chest rise slowly and easily beneath his grey t-shirt. I recalled our first meeting, and the ones that followed. Before turning to leave, I pulled the note from my back pocket and laid it on the small table next to his bed.

Hi Noah –

I'm heading home tomorrow morning very early so I will not get the chance to say goodbye in person. It was great to meet you. You're a very wise and courageous young man.

I look forward to seeing you again in the near future. Remember, you told me, 'I will get better.' I promise to do the same.

Until then, be well.

Jake (painter extraordinaire)

Later that evening I walked toward the main house to get on the bike and take a ride before the sun set. Brendan came out of the house holding a navy hat. "Got a little something for you." He handed me the hat.

"Thanks, Brendan." Taking the hat I admired the Jackrabbit logo on the back. "Does this mean I graduate?"

We laughed as he gave me a slap on the back. "You could think of it that way! Although there are many graduations in life, so don't think this is the only one."

"Yeah, right." I curled the brim of the hat between my hands and put it on backwards.

Brendan patted his leg, beckoning Canyon. "We're going to take a walk up the back trail, looks like Paul is going to make certain we get a beautiful sunset. Get a good night's sleep and I'll see you in the morning."

I watched the sun drop into the orange-blue sky as Brendan and Canyon began up the trail. As I reached for the bike I kicked Canyon's metal water bowl up against the house, the clang echoing off the sandstone walls. Brendan stopped and stood there looking at me until the dog looked too. He scratched Canyon's head, then spoke loudly, lifting his head in my direction to be sure I heard. "I don't know for sure, but I have a strong feeling that our friend there is going to be fine. What about you?"

I gave them a wave as Canyon barked in my direction, then both turned and continued up the path. I jumped on the bike and began pedaling away down the dirt road.

Early the next morning, I threw our bags into the back of my truck. The loops of green hose caught my eye. I grabbed it and carried it to a trash bin next to the house.

Brendan and I jumped into my pickup. He wore jeans, hiking boots, a long sleeve t-shirt and a brown fleece vest. "Now remember, Jake, we can take turns driving."

I nodded. "Thanks, but I feel pretty good. I'll let you know when I get tired." Four hours later we left the desert far behind and began climbing up I-70 and the Rockies toward Vail Pass. The temperature dropped into the 40s then 30s as the sparse, sandy landscape changed to snow-covered mountain peaks and deep drainages. Brendan nodded off a few times. I enjoyed the times the radio was off and we didn't talk, the tires humming and the wind buffeting at the pickup.

My mind wandered during one of these times as we rolled down a steep grade and Denver appeared in the distant haze. *Man, I can't believe I've been away this long. Gonna be weird going home, and trying to answer the questions that will come. I can hear them now. 'What are you going to do for work? How about Lauren, you gonna get married? Do you think you're over the accident?'* My mouth got dry and a pain grew in my stomach. *What am I gonna do?*

"Change the channel," a voice said.

"What?" I looked over at Brendan, but he was sleeping. And that's when I realized that I was replaying Preacher's advice in my head. *What you say to yourself is like a radio station. If you don't like what you're hearing, change the channel.* I thought over those questions that had been running through my mind and tried to put a positive spin on them. I had no doubt, now, that I could and would find answers to what I was going to do with my life. I knew I'd figure out my relationship with Lauren very soon. No, I wasn't "over" the accident, and in some ways hoped I never would be. I never wanted to forget Brian or the path that dealing with the accident had led me down.

Brendan took a deep breath through his nose and exhaled, opening his eyes and rolling his shoulders.

"So. How we doing? You getting tired? Want to grab a bite in Denver then I'll take over?"

"Sure, I could probably use a break."

"Perfect. I know a great taco stand on Sixth Avenue not far off the highway. That okay?"

I nodded.

"Good, we'll grab a bite, stretch a bit. And remember, any time during the drive, if you want, we can talk about how you'll continue applying what we all offered to you."

It's almost like he knew what I was thinking. "I'd appreciate that." Brendan gazed out the windshield, perhaps looking for a "Jackrabbit."

Brendan had removed his vest and was comfortably behind the wheel as we were back on I-70 heading toward the flat horizon of Kansas. It was good to be in the passenger seat; I slid off my shoes, and put my seat back. Later that night we checked into a hotel just off the highway and got a good night's rest.

We set out the next morning with Brendan in the driver's seat again and me sipping a steaming cup of coffee watching the fields and exit signs roll by.

I felt Brendan's glances and looked over. "What?"

"What? What?" he smiled, shifting his gaze quickly from me to the road ahead.

"Why are you looking at me like that?"

"Like what?" He laughed. "Alright, enough of this double-talk. Do you want to talk about what you're going to do in a few days when you get home?"

"Yeah, I'd like that. We need to."

"You know your growth couldn't take place in Utah. Back in Moab, you received information and knowledge. Out here…" Brendan swept his hand toward the rolling prairie, "you gain wisdom. Wisdom simply comes from applying what you're learning about Jackrabbit in your daily life. You know, experimenting with some new thinking and behavior. So, based on where you've been the past several months, where you are, and where you're going to be in three days, what's on your mind?"

I breathed deeply. "I'm scared. Well, first, I'm sad for Paul's family. Trust me; I know his soul is in a beautiful existence. I was there. In my mind, I think of it as being on Heaven's front porch. My soul was there, and I knew there was further to go. But then I backed off that porch and came back to Earth. And now that I'm going back home, where all the bad stuff started, I'm nervous… scared."

Brendan nodded.

"I'm scared about all the decisions I need to make, about work, and Lauren, Steve, everything. It's like my life has just been unpacked after sitting in a box a long time, and now I've got to face what's in there. I just don't want to go backward."

"Then focus on forward." We accelerated past a truck and settled back into the right lane. Brendan looked at me. "So what's your vision for work?"

"Well, I've been thinking about going back to work with Steve. I know my mom and everyone else is gonna think I'm crazy, but I just can't stop thinking that not long ago he had a great business going. Now his brother—his partner—is gone, and me, his main helper, I'm out on workman's comp. I'd like... I'd like to help him out, at least until he can get his business in good shape. I think I owe him that much."

"And what about after that?"

"Well, I think I want to explore the idea of becoming a teacher. Maybe even go back to school to learn about teaching. I've always thought about teaching, but never pursued it. I also wondered if maybe I could pursue teaching in organizations, you know learning and development or corporate education and training. The teaching... helping other people learn, like you do... that feels like it would be authentic work for me, something that fits who I am and what I want to contribute in the world."

"Sure sounds like a possibility. I've done a lot of work in that arena over the years."

There was something else to chat with Brendan about, but I was nervous and not sure if I should bring it up. After we rolled past another barn and grain silo, I turned. "You know Brendan, there is one more thing. I talked with Paul before he left and mentioned that I'd maybe like to speak to people about Jackrabbit, about what you help people learn. I know I'm really new at this, but something feels right to me about Jackrabbit. I'm pretty sure it's gonna help me. And I think it could help a lot of other people. It's kind of weird talking about Paul and how we'd seen him just a few days ago…" I paused "…and now we're off to say goodbye to him."

Brendan pursed his lips together before responding. "Yeah, weird. Sounds like a good idea, though, you talking about Jackrabbit. And don't worry about not being an expert. None of us are. We keep learning. And remember there are a lot of us… even beyond the people back in Moab, who can be part of your support system. Anything you need help with right away, or do you think you understand the philosophy behind Jackrabbit? It really is quite simple. I've got materials I could let you use when you start."

I turned again to Brendan. He looked like an aging movie star, his sunglasses atop his head, resting in his thick, gray hair. "Yes, I think I know it—I just need to get better at living it. But there is one thing, Brendan. What if people don't want to hear this, or they don't find the value in adopting the principles of Jackrabbit? Preacher said his buddies would make fun of him. What do I do if that happens?"

Brendan braked at the red lights glowing in front of us. "Jake, I learned a very long time ago that a sure recipe for failure is trying to please everyone. I did not develop Jackrabbit for people who don't want it. I developed it because I needed it. And then I found others who told me they needed it, too." Brendan winked, scanning my face for understanding.

I nodded my head slowly as a smile came to my face. "Got it."

"So, good. It seems like you've begun to develop a vision around your work. And do you have some actions to take when you get home?"

"Sure do. I'm gonna call Steve, then sit with my mom and dad and tell them my plan to go back with him and to pursue some teaching leads. I need to call the university near my house to schedule an interview to see about courses and credits and all that. I'm also going to call my brother's friend who's been working in the corporate education field."

"Great. That's the key—vision and action. And what about Lauren, any vision there?"

"Not sure, I am really confused. I mean I love her, she's great, but—"

Brendan interrupted, raising his hand to me as we slowed to an almost stop as a construction arrow blinked up ahead. "Let's try this. What if you and I don't speak with one another for three years and one night you walk out onto the Schooner behind the Lobster House, and I'm sitting there having a beer. I ask you about Lauren. What would you say?"

I exhaled long and loudly. "I can think of two very different answers." Brendan nodded for me to continue. "First, I could say that I think Lauren is doing fine, but I haven't seen her in a few years. I could say that my brother saw her in a bar recently and she was with another guy and seemed like she was doing okay."

"And the other answer?"

"I could say that Lauren and I are doing great, as a matter of fact she's in the ladies room and will be back in a moment. We worked through some stuff and got married two years ago, and had a baby last year."

Brendan waved as we passed a construction worker who guided us to another lane. "Yes, you could probably answer either way. Which one feels better?"

I rubbed my chin, and turned to look out my window. After a moment I looked back to him. "Definitely the second." I could hear the conviction in my own voice.

His face was neutral. "So what's your action with Lauren when you get home?"

The sun's glare sat in the side mirror out my window. I thought of asking Brendan to stop soon—I needed to stretch and use the bathroom. "I'll give her a call to see if I can stop by, I don't want to show up unannounced. She'll hopefully say yes, and then I'll grab some flowers and go over there and talk. I owe her some apologies... and explanations." I sighed. "Although I'm not sure exactly what I could say to explain everything that's happened to me. And I'm not sure she'll be willing to listen. I may have burned that bridge one too many times."

Brendan's eyes never left the road. "There aren't any guarantees that her vision will match yours. It's a gamble, Jake. But at least you know what actions you need to take."

Later that day, we pulled into the parking lot of a hotel in Columbus, maple leaves scuttling across the parking lot. The afternoon sun was dropping through tall, half-barren trees. Later, we drove to Maureen's house and spent time with her and some of Paul's family. At about ten p.m. we hugged and said we'd see them at the church in the morning.

We arrived at St. Francis Church early, but already the shiny, black funeral cars were lined up at the curb. Several small groups of people lingered out front and a man in a grey suit stood off to the side on a brick walk smoking a cigarette.

I left Brendan as he chatted with someone I didn't know, and pulled open the large wooden door at the rear of the church and entered. People were spread about in pews. Two small, older ladies wearing black lace on their heads were lighting candles in front of a statue. At the end of the long marble aisle, the altar sat surrounded by dozens of flower arrangements. Red and white roses, carnations, wild flowers, and white lilies sat in vases on the floor and several small tables.

Brendan came up next to me. "So, here we are."

"Yeah, here we are."

"How are you feeling?"

"Sad." I hadn't looked at him, my eyes still fixed on the arrangements of flowers.

"Yeah, me too. Let's go see Father Monahan for a moment. I want to be certain about my role today."

"Do you know everybody around here?"

"Not everybody. But I've known Paul and his family a long time, and met Father Monahan on several occasions."

Father Monahan stood as we entered the Sacristy of the church. "Ah, Brendan, so good to see you, my friend. It's been too long." He wore all black except for the patch of white under his round face. He stood several inches taller than Brendan. They hugged, and he patted Brendan sharply on the back.

"Hello, Father, nice to see you again," said Brendan. "You look good."

The large man smiled. "Well, I do feel good," he rubbed his ample belly and chuckled. "But I should probably get serious about getting rid of a bit of this. So sad about our dear friend, but if anyone was ever prepared for this next chapter of his soul, it is Paul. He told me not two weeks ago how excited he was to go see you…" He turned to me. "And I guess this is Jake?"

I extended my hand. "Yes, Father. Nice to meet you."

He smiled warmly. "Yes. You too, Jake. Paul told me about you. He didn't want to leave his family, knowing the end was so near. But he felt it was something he had to do… wanted to do, and was glad to make the trip to Moab, although he told me he knew it would be the last time he saw you both. It's good that he got to go."

I recalled Paul's peaceful smile when we said goodbye at Brendan's place—then it made sense. "Yes, me too, Father." I was a surprised by Fr. Monahan's upbeat demeanor.

Brendan and Father Monahan took a few minutes to review the logistics of the day. I excused myself and took a seat near the front of the church. I knelt and prayed for a good amount of time, until the funeral director said the service was going to begin and the organist began to play *Let There Be Peace on Earth.* The sound of a beautiful pipe organ filled the old stone church and the casket was rolled up the aisle. Maureen and the other family members—all dressed in black—filed into the pews in front of me.

Turning around, I saw that the church was packed. People stood in the aisles, and the large wooden doors remained open as others peered in. Fr. Monahan led a wonderful mass; his style was warm and engaging and it was obvious he'd known Paul very well. The music was spectacular—harps, trumpets, and French horns accompanied the organ, and a woman's deep, rich voice filled the church and permeated my soul.

After Communion there was a pause until Brendan rose from the pew in front of me and made his way to the lectern. I still wasn't used to seeing Brendan in a beautiful navy suit, white shirt and purple tie, since all I'd ever seen him in were jeans and hiking boots or sandals. He spoke easily—with compassion, thankfulness and humor—about Paul and his family and their friendship.

"I've had the pleasure of meeting many of you, and others I've heard about from Paul over the many years of our friendship. Many of you know that developing vision—the ability to create and make real something that you first imagine—was a vital concept in Paul's life. Based on how Paul was always looking to help us all and coach us, some of you can probably relate to this all too well.

Laughter filled the church.

"I'm certain that Paul is with us now in spirit, he'll always be. There's a fine line between where he his—how he is—and where and how we are right now in this church. If he were to talk to us right now, he'd probably tell us to cry, then be happy and remember him here on Earth. I'm sure he'd quote his patron saint, Paul, who said in *Timothy*, chapter four, verses 6 to 16, 'My life is being given as an offering to God, and the time has come for me to leave this life. I have fought the good fight, I have finished the race, I have kept the faith.'"

Brendan paused and scanned the audience, seemingly making eye contact with each individual over the sniffling and soft rustling.

"Let me leave you—and me—us, with this. As I look around at all of you in this church and knowing Paul as I did... it's clear that you, all of you were..." His voice cracked and he took in a deep breath, "No, not were, you are his vision. We are all part of the life Paul imagined, then made real. And rest assured that he remains proud of his vision—all of us. Right now he's just watching from a different place.

"So in honor of our dear father, grandfather, uncle, and friend, I'll leave you with one question from Paul Britton." Brendan paused, moving some papers from the lectern to the shelf underneath it. He looked back up to all of us, gazing over the entire congregation. "What's your vision?'"

Absolute silence fell over the church, not a sob or sniffle as Brendan came down from the altar to Paul's casket, leaned over and kissed it.

Just then, God knows why, I recalled the quote about vision I'd been trying to remember after a conversation with Brendan many days before.

A vision without a task is but a dream,
a task without a vision is drudgery,
a vision and a task is the hope of the world.

I turned slowly and looked over my shoulder. The emotion on faces and in the eyes of the congregation was unlike any I'd seen in a large group. My mouth fell open and the hair on my neck stood as my gaze drifted to those standing against the back wall and finally rested on one person. My mind raced back to my time in Cape Hatteras and the grandfather figure who spoke with me about Villanova basketball—but left no footprints. There, in suit and tie, his hands clasped in front of him, stood a man I was nearly certain was Hank, the mystery man from North Carolina. Our eyes locked on one another. He gave me a nod before turning and walking out of the church. The final prayers were said, and the congregation followed the casket down the aisle as a beautifully rich voice sang *On Eagle's Wings*. I needed to get outside.

As I left, I scanned the crowd quickly but didn't see any familiar faces though I knew there were some there. Outside, I glanced toward the near intersection, and then a figure caught my eye. There he stood, leaning on a stone wall in front of the grade school. I wanted to run, but instead walked very quickly to him. It was Hank, the man… the presence? the ghost?…with the disappearing footprints that I'd met on the beach. It felt like ages ago, but was really only three weeks.

"Hey, Hank," I called. "Don't move. I need to talk to you."

I strode quickly to where he stood. "Who are you, really? Why are you here, and what was all that about at Cape Hatteras? How come you didn't leave any footprints? What's going on?"

The corners of Hank's mouth pulled up just slightly into something resembling a smile. He reached for my hands. His eyes held peace and love and understanding as they connected to mine. "Jake, you know what's going on. Go with it. Be not afraid. Rest assured that Paul is with his Maker." He clasped my hands a moment, smiled for real, and then let go and walked away. As he turned the corner down a slight hill, I watched until his black hat disappeared beneath the top of a stone wall. Part of me wanted to take a few steps and look around the corner, but for some reason I didn't. I didn't need to. I knew. I don't think I could've moved anyhow.

I found Brendan, and we drove to Mo's house, where a huge crowd gathered. Kids were running everywhere, and people were hugging, and laughing, and crying, and looking at pictures, and eating, and telling stories about Paul and Ginny.

I'd finally seen Sammy, Bennie, Vanessa, Preacher, and Tim at the church, but not had a chance to talk with them. As I crossed the kitchen toward them, I saw that Sammy looked stunning. Her hair was down and she wore a sophisticated black dress, a simple silver cross hanging from her neck. "Hi, Jake, how are you," she said. "Beautiful ceremony, wasn't it?" I hugged her.

"Sure was. I'll never forget it." We leaned against the granite counter. "I'm going home tomorrow. I was going to stop to see you before I left, but we had to get out of town quickly, plus Brendan said I'd see you here for sure. Sammy, I really want to apologize…"

She held up her hand. "Jake, no need. I think we know and it's okay. I've a feeling you and I are going to be very good friends for a long time, probably the rest of our lives. I know it sounds weird since we've not known one another long, but that's the way it happens when people come to stay with Brendan. I love you and you love me, and we're good." She tilted her head sideways. "Yes?"

I took a deep breath and hugged her again, speaking into her ear. "Yes, Sammy, we're really good. Thanks." We separated a little—but not completely—and I looked into her eyes. "You know I'm gonna be calling you...probably a lot."

She kissed my cheek. "I wouldn't want it any other way. You just may be calling L.A."

"Is that so?" I asked, as she looked across the room where Tim and Benny stood talking.

I'd just finished a small sandwich and was sitting on a wooden chair in the corner of the living room when Paul's granddaughter Kate, dressed in a dress and shiny black shoes came around the corner and climbed onto my lap.

"Hi, Jake. My Pop's in Heaven. Mom told me he's probably playing pirates with all the kids there."

I laughed at the wonderfully innocent thought. "I'll bet he is, Kate."

"You never answered my question." Her tone was demanding.

I was confused. "What question?"

"You know, the one I asked you when you first came to my house to see Pop. Would you be scared if you had to run from the giant?"

I thought back to the day that I first met Kate at the front door just steps from where we now sat. *Man, kids have some great memories. Maybe it's because they're so young and don't yet have tons of other stuff cluttering their heads. So much has happened since then.*

"Oh, that question." I smiled, relieved. "You know, Kate, it's a funny thing about giants. Most of the time when we see one, we begin to run to get away from it. Think about all the people and giants in your books. We keep running and running, and the giant keeps running and running—and nothing really changes." I leaned in and put my mouth right next to Kate's ear. "Kate, the next time a giant is chasing you, you know what I want you to do?"

"Nope." Her face was serious as I pulled back, but I stayed just inches from her beautiful little face.

I looked right into her dark eyes. "I—and Pop too—want you to stop running. Kate, you turn around and look right at that giant and tell him 'I am finished running. I'm going down the beanstalk right now.'"

She thought for a moment. "What will the giant do then?"

"Nothing, he'll be gone."

Kate looked away for a moment, and then back at me. "Cool." She kissed my cheek before she grabbed another cookie off the table, took a bite and disappeared around the corner.

"Yeah." I smiled as my eyes welled. "Cool."

I rose and went in search of my new friends to say goodbye. I was surprised by how sad I was about leaving people I'd known for such a short time, but eager to go back to my home and family. We all promised to stay in touch, a polite social phrase that— with this group—I was sure everyone meant. I found Brendan standing outside talking to people I didn't know. He excused himself from the group and came over to shake my hand.

"You leaving?"

"Yep. I've got to get on the road. I'm gonna drive a few hours now, and then finish the trip tomorrow. I wanted to say thanks... and goodbye... before I left."

"It was a pleasure getting to know you, Jake. I know we'll be talking soon. And I know you'll be okay. You still got that paper?"

I patted my back pocket and felt the folded paper with my Jackrabbit scrawls. "Wouldn't be caught without it, Brendan. Never again. You have a safe trip back to Utah.... And be well, okay?"

Brendan reached in for a hug. "You too, Jake."

The next morning I pulled into the driveway of my mom and dad's house. I stepped down from my pickup and into my vision. I paused on the front porch, looking down the street at the golf course. After a moment, I turned to go inside and was met with the beautiful, teary-eyed face of my mom at the front door.

24

Alive Again

"Life is the proving ground of an evolving soul."
—Will Craig, author

Much time has passed since Jake pulled into his parents'
driveway. Are you wondering what happened? I've seen Jake
many times over these past years, although he never saw me.
He's done okay, and though there were difficult times, he never
did buy another hose.

It's me, Hank. I had to make an appearance, as it's such a
big day for Jake. I'm waiting for him now, sitting at a picnic table
on a beach by the Cape May wetlands, not far from the famous
lighthouse. It's a cool fall afternoon and the surf is mesmerizing.

Appropriately, I'm reading the most recent edition of *Exit Zero* magazine.

Jake's coming my way now. I see him walking quickly down the beach wearing his navy blue PENN sweatshirt. I tug down the brim of my baseball cap, push my sunglasses up my nose, and look down again at the magazine. After Jake's shadow passes by, I loudly clear my throat. Jake's pace slows and he glances back in my direction, then he stops as if he's walked into fresh cement.

"Hank?" he says. I look up and smile. Jake shakes his head, returns the few steps, then slides onto the bench across from me. "Shit, it is you."

"Hello, Jake, of course it's me. Who were you expecting? Elvis? Sinatra?"

Jake takes a deep breath and looks toward the ocean then back to me. "What, what…I mean, why are you here? What's wrong?"

"Nothing. Everything's fine, Jake." He's just staring at me, wearing a confused look. "You look good after all these years. A few gray hairs, but otherwise not bad."

"Yeah, I'm kind of thinking the same thing, except you look exactly the same, Hank. I mean *exactly*."

I laugh. "One of the perks of the job, Jake. You have a few minutes to get caught up?"

"Well, sure, but only a minute. I'm meeting Sammy at the VFW Hall. She said she needed help getting set up for a fund-raiser being held there later this week."

I know that's not the real reason for Sammy's request, but just nod and say, "Yes, I know. Don't worry, she's okay."

Jake leans his head back, staring to the sky. "You know about me meeting Sammy?" he says, glancing in my direction. He lets out a big breath and then looks out at the ocean. "I had a feeling something weird was gonna happen today. This is, what, only the third time I've seen you in my life? First at that beach in North Carolina... then at Paul's funeral... and now."

Removing my sunglasses, I look at Jake intently. "Well, you may have only seen me three times, but I've seen you a lot more often. That's just how it works. You've never been alone, Jake, even if you felt that way."

Jake returns my gaze, slowly realizing what I'm talking about. His expression gets somber. "You were there, weren't you? That time in the kitchen when I was looking at that knife and thinking how nice it would be to end all the pain?"

"Of course."

"Wow, so it was you?" Jake said. "It makes sense now, I felt something, even with the fear I had, the anxiety...I felt something...I felt you. You were with me." Jake's eyes become glassy, and he wipes them with the sleeve of his sweatshirt. "And that other time..."

I interrupt him. "Hold that thought a minute, Jake. There's someone else coming who wants to see you."

We turn as a man with broad shoulders and dark hair walks towards us. Jake recognizes him almost immediately.

"Oh my God, what is happening, Hank?" Jake turns to me then looks back at the approaching figure. "That's Benny, right? But... but he died years ago, in that plane crash. With Noah's mom and dad. When I got that call, I almost lost it. If I hadn't reached out to Preacher..."

"I know, Jake. Yes, it's Benny. Remember talking about the fine line between *here* and *there*? He can be both at the moment, just like me."

"Benny, man. I can't believe you're here," Jake says as the figure arrives at my table. "I'm so sorry about the crash. I prayed so much for you and the others, and Noah."

Benny nods then reaches out to rest his hand on Jake's shoulder. "I know, Jake, I know. We got your prayers."

Benny looks to me then back at Jake. "I hope you don't mind, but I asked Sammy to meet us here rather than wait at the VFW Hall. I thought it would be easier here than in a more public place."

At that moment, we hear Sammy's voice. We turn and see her waving at us as she jogs down the beach, her ponytail flowing behind her.

She gives Jake a hug then pulls away, holding his face in her hands. "You good with all this?" Jake smiles, though he has tears in his eyes.

Sammy moves to my side of the table and bends down, placing her arms around my neck, "Hi, Hank." She also hugs Benny.

"Sammy...you know Hank? Why, why are you not surprised or freaking out about seeing Hank or Benny here?" says Jake.

Sammy takes Jake's hands. "Jake, we've been together for quite a few years now and there were so many times I wanted to tell you, but wasn't sure if I should or how to or, or... well I was just so confused.

"But you're *here*, right? You're alive?" Jake replies slowly, emphasizing the word *here*.

"Oh yeah, Jake, yes, I'm here. I'm really alive."

"But then, what's happening?"

I invite everyone to sit at the table. After they are settled, I say, "Jake, Sammy and I know one another, and so do Benny and me. We've known one another for a long time."

Jake looks at Sammy then Benny. He pulls off his base-ball cap—the one with the jckrbbt logo, of course. "Benny, you know Hank?" Benny smiles slightly and nods. "Even, even before the plane crash?" says Jake. Again, the smile and nod.

Jake turns to Sammy, "And you? How long"

"A long time, Jake. Hank first showed up for me when I was about 14, then again early in my Wall Street career, and a few times after that." Jake shakes his head then runs his fingers through his hair. He looks to Benny and me and we just smiled.

Sammy paused. "Yes, Hank's my guy."

"Mine, too," says Benny.

Jake looks at me and I nod, then add, "And the others, too."

"The others?" asks Jake in a frustrated tone.

"Yes, Jake," says Sammy. "Learning and living the principles of jackrabbit isn't easy. All of us need a support system. Counting you along with me, Benny, Brendan, Preacher, Noah, and our friend, Paul it's seven in all."

Jake rubs his face, and places his head in his hands, elbows resting on the table. He looks to the three of us, then to me. "You knew...you know them all?"

"Will I see Paul?" Jake turned to Benny. "I mean if you're here, others could be here to, right? Why not Paul?"

Benny looked to me, with a flip of his head as if to say, *you answer.*

I smiled and replied to Jake, "Oh, he's got his own seven now."

Jake looked to the blue sky, talking to none of us directly, "No shit," he chuckled, "Of course he does."

I nod, then stand. "While it's great to sit here and reminisce, I think Sammy and Jake have some work to do. So I guess we should be going."

Benny stands first. "I have to get going, but I just wanted to say hi. Take care, Jake. Don't lose that vision and focus of yours. You've come a long way, but your life ain't over yet."

Jake stands up and gives Benny a bear hug, then steps back. "Thanks, man. Luv ya."

Sammy stands and joins Jake as they head down the beach. Benny heads the other way, then disappears over a small dune. I decide to follow Jake and Sammy, sure they won't notice me. As I reach them, I start to pick up on their conversation.

Sammy sighs then says, "It's always good to get back here. We should go to The Schooner for lunch tomorrow if it's still open this late in the season."

"Great idea," says Jake. "That's one of my favorite places in Cape May, actually, one of my favorites anywhere."

"Sometimes I still find it hard to believe that the post-Wall Street part of my life began there when I met Paul's wife Ginny and we sipped glasses of wine. I remember it as clearly as if it were yesterday, but it was more than 20 years ago."

"I hear ya," replies Jake. "I've been in a reflective mood lately, guess it's that birthday thing. Tomorrow's a big one for me."

"I haven't forgotten," says Sammy. "Maybe it's why I'm doing a lot more reflection myself these days, too. Remember, I'm a little older than you." Sammy holds her finger and thumb very close together as she emphasized the word *little*.

Jake nods, "Yeah, just a little."

They are both silent for a few moments.

"Before we get to the Hall, let's talk business a little, OK?" says Sammy. Jake nods.

"OK, so the movie," she says. "Here's where we are. The financing is in place, thanks in large part to your friends, and we've got the production schedule and budget pretty well finalized. All we need to do is get two more actors in place. For that supporting female role I'm pretty certain we can get...."

The sound of crickets interrupts, and Jake reaches into his pocket and pulls out his iPhone.

A young woman appeared on his screen to facetime. "Oh, hey Kate, what's up? I'm here with Sammy." Kate looks a lot like her Grampa Paul.

The three chat for a while about Kate's progress in finding an actress to fill the last role in the group's latest film. "I was jogging on the beach and almost ran into that actress we've been pursuing. At first, I was scared to go up to her, and I know she's only a person, like us, but she's, she's …well know who she is. Then I hear Jake's voice in my head saying, 'stop running, and the giant will be gone.' So I introduced myself and she's interested!"

I tune out at that point, but continue following Jake and Sammy. A few minutes later they hang up the phone then turn to head up towards Cape May VFW Post 386. When they get close to the Hall, I hurry ahead so I can sneak in a back door and watch as they enter. Contrary to what Jake thinks, the inside is already decorated, and it's not for a fundraiser. Streamers are hung all over and colorful balloons are tied to chairbacks and wall sconces. Large number 5s and 0s are everywhere. The room is crowded with people. I hadn't seen their cars, so they must have parked on the side streets. A woman moves to the middle of the room, yelling, "Quiet, quiet here they come."

The door opens slowly and Sammy enters, sunlight spilling in around her. She steps aside quickly as everyone shouts in unison, "Surprise!"

Jake jumps, but then is soon engulfed in a hug from his wife Lauren and their three kids. He smiles and laughs, hugging and kissing people who join the queue. "You got me," he yells to Sammy and Lauren.

An hour later, I'm sitting on a barstool and pivot so my back is to the bar. Jake notices me, then raises his hands as if to say, "What the…?" I raise my fingers in the sign of peace and flash him a smile. I swing back to the bar, ask for a beer, and start to watch the football game. Soon, I hear Jake's voice.

"I can't believe you," he says as he slides onto a stool next to me.

I nod to the bartender who puts a bottle in front of Jake. "I decided to make one last appearance," I say.

"Yeah, great timing. And on the exact day of my surprise 50th birthday party."

"Wouldn't have missed it for the world. … Jake, I know you're busy here getting caught up with all your friends and family, but let me take a minute to say I'm proud of you. You had a pretty rough time after the accident, and you carried it with you a long time." I pause then add, "Too long."

Jake takes a swig of his beer. An older man I recognize as his uncle pats him on the back as he passes by. "I did carry it too long. I'd be thinking I was making great progress, using jckrbbt to achieve my vision… but then suddenly I'd feel overwhelmed, like I didn't deserve to be happy. Now I'm finally getting to acknowledge that that's just the way life is…it just unfolds…even with the pain and the suffering and all the bullshit. You just have to work your way through it and get to the other side. It's all about resilience."

I could tell the past was pulling Jake under again "And get out of blame and regret and judgment. You just can't get any momentum with all that around."

He looks at me, then says, "I was actually doing pretty good until a few years ago when my buddy Steve got sick. He was there when the accident happened, so he was the only one I could really talk to about it. And then he left us…way too young. His death brought the accident and all those confused feelings back with more intensity."

"I know," I say. "It was good that you went to see Brendan during that time. I know he helped you again by getting back to the basics of jackrabbit."

"He sure did, and so many others too. One thing I've learned is you have to seek support when the storms of life roll in. And you have got to put yourself first and get your head right before you can get going again. It all gets better then."

Lauren arrives carrying two plates piled high with food. She places them in front of us, and then, rubbing Jake's back, says, "Thought you and your friend might be hungry. You're on the move talking with everyone, and I didn't want you to not eat." She turns to me and reaches out her hand. "Hi, I'm Lauren."

Smiling, I shake her hand, "Yes, I know my dear." I turn to Jake and laugh at his expression which I interpreted as *She can see you? Shit, who do I tell her you are?* I nod reassuringly.

"Honey, this is Hank," he finally manages to say.

She smiles. "Well, hi, Hank. Glad you could make it Jake's party, it's nice to…." She tilts her head, scrunches her nose, and turns slightly to Jake. "Hank? THE Hank?" Without waiting for a response, she puts her arms around me. "Thank you," she whispers.

A new voice interrupts us. "Hey, old man, pretty good surprise." Jake's younger son grabs his dad, placing him in a headlock, as his older brother joins in. Jake's daughter stops them. "Hey, hey, let my Daddy go. You could hurt an old person like him." The old-age jokes continue, then he introduces me to all the kids, although I'd know them since before they were born. Jake and Lauren's love and pride for them was wonderful to experience. After a few minutes Lauren and the three kids head back towards the rest of the crowd.

"You sure are blessed with that gang," I say.

Jake nods. "Sure am. I remember in the Outer Banks when I saw that guy surfing with his sons, and thought about the possibility of me ever being a dad." Jake pauses, taking a deep breath of emotion. "And now I've taken those guys surfing just a few blocks from here many times. It's really kind of crazy when you think about it."

I just smile. "Or not."

Jake sips his beer, toasting a few guys across the bar. "Right. You get what you focus on. I know when Charlie, our oldest, was born, I really felt overwhelmed for a while. It was only a year after Lauren and I got married, and two years after I left Moab."

We hear a commotion and both turn to see an older man on a purple scooter headed our way, his long gray hair pulled into a ponytail. Preacher.

"Well," I say, "I was wondering when you might grace us with your presence."

"Ha, that's enough out of you already," he replies. "Keep it up and I may have to straighten you out." He pulls his scooter closer, not paying any attention to many toes he nearly runs over on his way.

I look to Jake, who's wearing a priceless expression. "And this guy," Preacher says, pointing his thumb at Jake, "what's with all the gray hair?" Jake smiles and leans down to embrace Preacher, who holds him tightly.

We chat for about 10 minutes as Preacher retells the stories of how he and I met and how I'd spent time with him in jail on several occasions.

"I'm gonna go get some grub," Preacher finally says, backing up his scooter and turning toward the food table. "I'll catch up with you both again later." As he rolls away, we see the bumper sticker on back of his scooter: *Caution! This scooter has been known to run people over.*

Jake laughs then rises and says, "I think I'd better go mingle. You sticking around?"

I nod. "Yep. I'll be here for a while yet."

Jake moves back to the crowd. He stops by a while later with the wives and children of his two friends, Brian who had died in the accident and Steve who had more recently passed on. They were all doing so well and had certainly carried on with courage after the loss of their husbands and fathers. I was happy Jake stayed in touch with them and they cared for one another. Often in life, tragedy weaves a strong bond.

Toward the end of the party, I decide to join Lauren, Sammy, Jake's mom and some others at a table near the door. Lauren introduces me as a friend of Jake's. The front door opens and Jake comes in, returning after escorting some old friends to their car. Right behind him is an older man wearing an untucked denim shirt with a full head of gray hair accompanied by a much younger man about six-foot, two inches with broad muscular shoulders and a narrow waist, dreadlocks pulled back into a ponytail.

People in the room start to whisper and point to the younger man. I smile. Brendan and Noah have arrived.

Jake greets them first, commenting on Noah's amazing transition from the young boy in a wheelchair twenty years ago to a pro football player. He guides the pair to the buffet table then back to our table where he makes introductions.

Two small boys in Philadelphia Eagles jerseys make their way to the empty table next to us, and shoot pleading looks at their Uncle Jake, who nods and asks Noah if it's OK if the boys come over. Noah waves at the boys then takes out a sharpie and signs each of their jerseys on one of the same white numbers that he wore on many Sundays.

Preacher moves his scooter closer to our table and looks at the boys. "Want me to sign too?" he asks. The boys look confused, and then back away, leaving us all for a good laugh.

Jake smiles at Noah, "Thanks. My nephews absolutely love you. But I must say I'm surprised to see you. I mean with the Dallas game next week."

Noah finishes chewing a bite of his sandwich, then smiles. "All good. We had a strong week of practice and since this is our bye week I got cleared to come and celebrate with you. Plus," he turns to Sammy, "also a great chance to see my mom." Sammy returns his smile.

Jake's mom is looking confused, so I lean over and whisper, "Sammy adopted Noah after his parents died in that plane crash with Benny."

"So, the big 5-0. How's it feel?" Brendan asks.

Jake shakes his head. "Not sure. It's been a long journey getting here and I'm kind of still taking it all in. How about you?"

"Well, doctors said the surgery went better than expected. I had a scan and blood work last week and all good. Just one day at a time, right, Jake?"

"Yep, sure helps to hold useful thoughts."

Brendan continues, looking to each of us as he spoke. "Not sure how many more times we'll be together. I want you all to know how much I love you, and am thankful for the wonderful work you've done and are doing in our world. There are many people who need us and the work we offer them."

He turns to Jake. "Celebrating your 50th is a gift. You arrived in Moab a long time ago as one beat down human being, and here you are. With your writing, and speaking and movies," he nods to Sammy, "with this talented lady, you've taken tragedy and used it for good...a lot of good. Thank you, Jake. I'm proud of you and what you've done."

No one speaks; there is no need. The smiles and misty-eyed looks we all share with one another say it all. A small group of people doing our best to support others on this wonderful journey called life.

Lauren rises, and says, "C'mon, Jake. We've got to start cleaning up. You're no longer the featured celebrity. It's time to earn your keep and help me carry some things to my car." I get up, too, saying I'll come along and help.

Jake and I grab boxes and bags. As we exit the Hall, the large full moon casts a brighter light than is normal for nighttime. Lauren is well ahead of us as we follow to the end of the block then start to turn a corner. As we do, we see a figure approaching.

Jake looks to me. "Mixing up *here* and *there* again?" he says. I don't reply, and just turn back to the figure.

The man stops in front of us. He's wearing khakis and has a white t-shirt peeking out of his navy V-neck sweater. "Hi, Jake," he says.

Jake is biting his bottom lip. He drops his bags and lurches to hug the man tightly. He lets out a few sobs. "Paul," he manages to croak.

"Yes, it's me. Live and in person." Paul pauses. "Well, maybe not in person," he adds, winking at me.

"I didn't think I'd ever see you again," says Jake.

"Well, nothing would keep me from seeing you today. Plus, Benny needed me today for someone he's working with. You look good, Jake, and I'm guessing today was a lot of fun."

"It really was." Jake stands there, staring at Paul. "I can't believe it's you. Even after all that's happened today, I just can't believe it. I'll always remember you coming out of that wave so many years ago."

Paul patted Jake's shoulder, "Yes, it was a wonderful chance meeting. Or not so much." Paul nods to me. "It was this guy that told me to be sure to go bodysurfing on that beach that morning."

"Really, it was you, Hank?" Jake asks me.

"Yes, it was me that told Paul, but not just me. Ginny told me to tell him."

Jake stands motionless, his head shaking slowly and tilting to one side. "Wait," he says looking at me then to Paul, "Your wife Ginny, who passed a year before we met, she…she made all of this happen?"

Paul smiles, "Seems that way, I told you she was special, didn't I?"

"Damn, crazy," replies Jake. "All I know is I'm pretty sure I wouldn't be here today, if not for meeting you….and then the others."

"Well, Jake, we were happy to do our part and offer you jackrabbit, and then the rest was up to you. You had to grow and apply the principles," says Paul.

"I'd really love to talk more, but I've got to get going now, so you take care Jake," Paul adds.

"Paul, I know I'm not one of your seven," says Jake, "but will you do me a favor and keep an eye on me?"

Paul turns to me, shaking my hand, then turns back to Jake. "Absolutely my friend, absolutely."

Jake and I stand motionless as Paul turns and walks away, fading into the night. Jake then wipes his eyes, and we gather the bags and boxes and hurry to catch up with Lauren as she loads her car.

As we re-enter the Hall a few minutes later, Jake scans the room. I point out two last Mylar balloons moving back and forth gently. "Maybe those are just random balloons," I say, "but maybe it's your old friends come to pay their respects. I think they're happy that you're not just living any more, but you're alive."

Jake moves towards the balloons. "Hey you two, I was wondering if you'd show up." His eyes filled, his voice a whisper, "I'm good. Luv ya."

Discussion Questions

Chapters

Preview

1) Back to Life...The Path of Resilience. What do these words convey to you? When have you been "resilient" in your life? How did that resilience get you through that event?

2) What is your initial reaction to the book cover? Does anything in the description/title hook you?

3) What do you hope to gain from reading this book?

Chapter 1: Why did I have to come back?

- When have you felt "dead?" Was it a life/death situation? Was it an event where you just felt that your life was headed for a dead end?

- Have you ever lost someone and wondered how you would go on? How did you come back to life from this situation?

- When have you felt guilty when someone died? Have you ever felt helpless? How did you get past this? When did you realize there was nothing you could have done?

Chapter 2: Rock bottom is a hell of a place

- Have you ever felt a spiritual presence during a down time in your life? Did you tell anyone? How did they react?

- Were you firm in your belief that someone was there with you? How did you "explain it?" What was the presence "saying" to you? Did it help guide your direction? How?

- Have you ever felt so down and out that someone gave you a wake-up call? How did you feel? How did you respond?

Chapter 3: Run

- When have you felt misunderstood?

- When have you ever felt the need to run or escape? Where did you go? What did you do to shut people out? Did you read a book? Listen to music and close your eyes? Jump in the car and head to the shore/beach? Head to the mountains? Why was the place special for you?

- Did these escapes truly open your heart to move on from your problem?

- If you are religious or spiritual, when have you doubted "God"—or how you might describe a higher power? For what have you "blamed" God? Did you feel as though he was a friend who let you down? Did you repair that relationship? How did you repair that relationship? Did you act in the moment when you blamed him for your misfortunes?

Chapter 4: Date with a garden hose

- Look at the quote, "*Nothing is worth more than this day.*" What does the quote mean to you? How would this change your daily attitude if you said this quote every day?

- Have you ever arrived to your special place and realize that running away wasn't the answer?

Chapter 5: Open to where it may lead

- When have you ever spoken to a stranger, only to wonder, "How did this person come into my life?"

- Why is it easier to discuss issues with a stranger than with my own family or friends?

- Have you ever wondered about the coincidences that manage to make you think or help?

Chapter 6: Direction

- Have you ever met someone and felt an instant connection? Or you've met someone and you feel that something they said makes you think? Why did that person come into your life just when you needed them?

- How do you feel when people bring up God or religious aspects in a conversation? Are you willing to listen?

- When have you started to relax, when your pain comes back to you out of the blue in a surreal way?

- How did it make you feel to go back to that place from where you tried to escape?

Chapter 7: Homecoming

- When has the stress of life gotten to you so much that you begin to imagine if it is real or in your mind? Did you find any clarity? Were you more confused than ever? When did you realize you need to go back and face your issues?

- What led you to realize that running away or trying to escape is not the way to get away from your problems? That facing your problem is the only way? Did you start to relive your decisions?

- Have you ever looked at your life and realized that it isn't quite how you thought it was?

- When have you tried to avoid friends? When did you "click" and realize you needed to reconnect?

Chapter 8: Lauren

- Did you ever say or do something that you know you had to do for yourself, even though someone may have been hurt? Could you have done or said anything differently?

- How were you pulled in different directions?

Chapter 9: A momentary lapse of reason

- When the time comes to move on or make a change, have you ever had that momentary lapse of reason? Should I stay? Should I continue?

- Perhaps you felt split in two; you were eager for the adventure, but apprehensive at the thought of actually making this happen. Why did you choose to move on?

- Have you resorted to prayer to get you through? How did that feel?

- Once you decided to move on, have you ever been hit with a loss that made you wonder if you could continue?

- Did you ever think you were to blame for a ruined relationship? What did you do to make sure you continued on your path?

Chapter 10: Population 4,700

- When have you started toward a new experience, or adventure, only to have panic set in?

- When have you been unsure of which direction to turn?

- Take a moment to think: What invigorates you when you just need a break?

- Finish this sentence. I wish I was more like ___ because ___. What characteristics do you admire in that person? Are they qualities you lack?

- When Jake enters Sammy's he noticed a sign on the bar wall. It brought a smile to Jake's face. He committed the sign quote to memory. In this day of memes and endless on line quote posts, what quotes do you remember? Why do they impact you?

- During the conversation with Jake, Sammy states, "Sometimes we need to make some wrong turns in life to get on the right road."

- When has life dealt you some "wrong turns?" How did you get back on the right road of life? What led you back to the right path?

- How has "thinking" helped you to move on from a situation?

- Have you ever listened, really listened to others and try to help them, simply because you had a different perspective? When have you been a "philosopher?"

- Brendan asked Jake a simple question, which led Jake to question himself, his decisions. *Why are you here? Why ARE we here? What is YOUR purpose?*

- Jake went on his way, purchasing the beer, not the vodka. He discussed the fact that he drank too much, and was glad he was able to resist the vodka. A start indeed. It is important that we make a start. And then the small steps begin. When has something similar happened to you?

Chapter 11: Vision vs. reality

- Have you ever been able to shift your focus? ... Have you ever had a day when you think, "Nothing is going right?" And from that moment on, everything goes wrong? Did you look for trouble to make your "prediction" come true? What if you shifted your focus and thought, "This is going to be a great day!" Picture it. If something goes wrong, think, "It's only a little bump in the road." Perhaps you are stuck inside on a foul weather day. What if you decided to use the time to complete something you have wanted to do for a long time? When have you turned the proverbial lemons into lemonade? What change do you need in your life?

- Have you developed a vision? What do you need to do to make that happen? Develop a plan. Create reality. How can you make this happen?

Chapter 12: Jackrabbit

- Notice the quote in the beginning of the chapter. What do you think the author means when he states that life's purpose always points in the right direction?

- What is your purpose? Are you still heading in that direction?

- Jake later changes his mood when a "rich guy" passes by. Brendan continues talking about some rich who give in different ways. Do you have to be "rich" monetarily in order to give to others? What riches or talents can you share? Which riches or talents have you shared? What motivates you to want to share with others?

- The jackrabbit is the image Brendan used to provide an image to vision. What image would you give yourself, to describe the type of person you are? Why would you choose this symbol?

Chapter 13: Be still

- Once again, the author includes his own quote. Why do we enjoy the quiet of the mountains, the opening of a new day, or the gentle swoosh of the ocean rolling in and out? There is a peacefulness that gives a new perspective on the day.

- When have you blocked out the noise of the television, computer, or traffic? How did it affect you? Did you gain new perspective?

- Have you ever gone into a church, and just sat listening? How did it make you feel?

- When have you felt the need to slow down? How does slowing down provide clearer focus?

Chapter 14: Sammy's story

- Have you ever met someone and wondered why they were sent into your life at just the right time?

- What about the "seven degrees of separation?" When have you met someone who knows someone...? Have you ever wondered how that person wound up in your life just then?

- When have you kept a reminder of a special event, or a quote that made an impact on you Why did you keep it? What memories or meaning does it evoke?

Chapter 15: Confession

- How many times in your life have you ever thought, *"What if?"* What if I ____ instead of ____...? Did it ever change the outcome?

- When have you felt God's presence? Or a spiritual presence? Did you ever ask God to help others? How did it make you feel?

Chapter 16: Change of plans

- When meeting someone special you haven't seen in a while, how do you feel? What happens when you meet them again? How do you greet them?

- When have you had to make a choice between right and wrong? How did you respond?

Chapter 17: An uncomfortable night

- When have you decided on a path only to start doubting the outcome? Do negative thoughts reenter your mind?

- How do you begin to shake the thoughts out of your mind?

Chapter 18: Being still with myself

- When have you tried to relax, whether at home, or at work, but the noise just keeps entering your thoughts?

- When have you had to practice something over and over until it is right?

- How well do you know yourself? Have you ever stopped to think about what you know about yourself? What is the best thing about you? What makes you truly happy? How can that help you with the rest of your life?

- When have you changed yourself in order to please others?

- When have you ever settled in your life?

- Have you ever been let down after a much-anticipated event where you paid a lot of money and thought, "What a waste?"

- Have you ever attended an event with friends that didn't cost much, but you enjoyed it more than you thought you would? What was the draw to the simple event?

- Who do you love? Why do you love them? What is love? How are you called to love?

Chapter 19: Getting unstuck

- When have you been unhappy, only to find yourself blaming others, rather than looking inside yourself to find out how you might need to change? Is it the way you look at things? Do you focus on the negative, rather than the positive? Once you focus on the positive, have you ever felt like the Little Engine that could? *I think I can, I think I can.* Before you know it, do you feel your attitude changing for the better?

- Evolve. The change has begun. Does it happen overnight, or can you take things one small step at a time? How do you envision each new day?

- As discussed before, have you looked at things anew from someone else's perspective?

- Paul speaks to Jake and asks the question, *"If you were to go to sleep tonight knowing that you won't wake in the morning, would you be content with how you spent today?"* How would you answer that question?

- If your answer was negative, what would you change? Look at those areas of discontentment.

- Have you ever lost focus as time passed? How did you get back on track?

Chapter 20: Chillaxin'

- Out of the mouth of babes. Have you ever had a child question you about something, and you weren't sure how to answer? How did you respond? When you answered the question, did the simplicity of the answer make you think about an issue that really had a simple solution?

- Faith. When have you felt overcome by faith? You believe with your whole heart that something will come true? When did that faith carry you through a difficult situation?

Chapter 21: Anything but alone

- Look at the author's quote that begins the chapter. How many times have you shut people out? Said you were "fine" when you really weren't?

- When did you realize that you can count on others to get you through? Who are the people you can count on to help you through good and bad times?

- Have you ever taken the easy way out, only to realize, you are getting nothing out of a situation?

- Do you pray? Do you pray alone? When do you find yourself praying? When you need something? What about when you just want someone to talk to?

- Have you ever thought of God as your friend? Do you thank God for each new day? A blank slate to begin anew?

Chapter 22: Moving on

- When have you been nervous about something and envision a positive result? Did you feel a sigh of relief that things will be better than you originally thought?

- When have you volunteered? Why did you volunteer? How did you feel when you finished? Why do you think that was so?

Chapter 23: The end of the beginning

- When have you experienced the loss of someone who influenced you? Despite the sadness and shock, how did that person affect you? Does their memory promote action to follow the lessons they have taught you? Why?

- Think about the serenity prayer. *God grant me the serenity to accept the things I cannot change, the courage to change the things I can, and the wisdom to know the difference.* How can you apply it in your life?

- You've envisioned the positive, and set a course of action. A few worries enter your mind. When is it time to move on? Why not start now?

- Can you live your vision, keep the faith, look at life from the eyes of a child, and keep in touch with your support group?

Chapter 24: Alive again

- Have you ever experienced a feeling of something, someone helping you, or providing comfort, yet you just can't explain it? Have you ever felt angels, or another being pulling you toward something? Are you still utilizing your support group?

- Sometimes, life has a way of repeating itself. When have you felt the need to return to what worked for you? When did you find the resilience needed to continue your vision and action plan?

- When have you realized that you can accept people's offers of help, but you need to take that first step, and continue to make your visions a reality?

- Keep the memories of those who have gone before you. When a feeling comes over you, and strong memories return, how do you know it isn't a lost loved one, showing their support? How did you feel after reading the last chapter?

The Jckrbbt Model

What did you think of Danny's *jckrbbt* model when you first saw it?

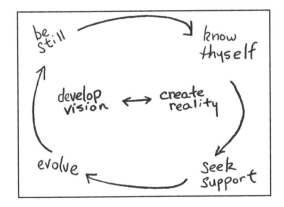

- How does it compare to other models you have seen and practice? Does it complement or contrast with them? How?

- Does this model help you be more fully ALIVE? Why or why not?

Post Reading

1) How has reading this book made you think about religion/spirituality in your life? Did it change your view on those subjects? If so, how?

2) The author begins each chapter with a quote. How did this quote add to each chapter? Which quote(s) affected you? Why?

3) What aspects of the *jckrbbt* principles do you envision applying in your life? Can you use any of the steps right now?

4) How do you achieve your goals? Do you have a plan?

5) How do you think the author promoted "self-help" guidance in the book?

6) What is your lasting impression of the book?

7) What did you like/dislike about the book? Are there any additional concepts you would like to have covered?

8) How have you changed since you read the book?

9) Why would you recommend this book to a friend?

10) Would you consider reading more books by this author?

Literary Questions

1) How does the book title relate to the content?

2) If you were to add illustrations to the book, what would you add? Why do you think they would enhance the content?

3) What feelings were generated when you read the book? Do any particular passages come to mind that contributed to these feelings?

4) How would you describe Jake?

5) Could you connect with Jake in any of the situations within the story?

6) With which character did you most connect? Why? Do you see yourself in any of the characters? Why? How?

7) How did Jake change throughout the story? Did you see any growth?

8) What themes did you find throughout the book?

9) What kind of conflicts did you find throughout the story?

(Man vs. self, Man vs. Man, Man vs. Nature, Man vs. Supernatural)

10) How were conflicts resolved?

11) If you could ask the author any questions, what would you ask him?

12) How did the last chapter affect you?

13) If a sequel to the book followed, what events should it cover?

About the Author

Danny Bader is a best-selling author and inspirational speaker whose life was transformed by a near death experience more than 20 years ago. His struggle to go from just living again to being engaged and alive was the basis for his fictional book, *Back To Life* (which is a second edition of his first book, *Back From Heaven's Front Porch*). He followed that up with *Abraham's Diner, Simple wisdom for more control, focus & inspiration*, and the 2018 release, *I Met Jesus for a Miller Lite*.

As a sought-after speaker, he routinely gives keynotes and leads workshops to the people of some of the largest organizations in the nation… ***inspiring others to live their best live***s. He's the creator and host of the BACK TO LIFE podcast.

www.dannybader.com

Back To Life Podcast:
    https://www.dannybader.com/podcast

https://www.facebook.com/danny.bader.7

https://www.instagram.com/_dannybader/

https://www.youtube.com/user/dannybader11

email: danny@dannybader.com

Made in the USA
Monee, IL
31 July 2023

40188502R00154